FIROS ISEU

Comrade Sao

*A former porridge cook of Samrong Temple
Prison, Battambang Province, during the
Khmer Rouge Regime in 1977*

AUSTIN MACAULEY PUBLISHERS™
LONDON • CAMBRIDGE • NEW YORK • SHARJAH

A CIP catalogue record for this title is available from the British Library.

ISBN 9781398496255 (Paperback)
ISBN 9781398496262 (Hardback)
ISBN 9781398496286 (ePub e-book)
ISBN 9781398496279 (Audiobook)

www.austinmacauley.com

First Published 2024
Austin Macauley Publishers Ltd
1 Canada Square
Canary Wharf
London
E14 5AA

I would like to dedicate this autobiography in memory of my parents, my family members and more than three million Cambodian people who perished during the Khmer Rouge regime for three years, eight months and twenty days from 17 April 1975 until 7 January 1979.

The following is a list of my family members on April 17, 1975:

Mrs Leav, age 75, born in 1900, grandmother

Iseu Yaristan, age 52, born 1923, father

Rabia Setamat, age 35, born in 1940, mother

Sina Iseu, age 19, born in 1956, sister

Farid Iseu, age 17, born 1958, brother

Rashid Iseu, age 15, born in 1960, brother

Firos Iseu, age 12, born in 1963, author

Farida Iseu, age 10, born in 1965, sister

Fuad Iseu, age 8, born in 1967, brother

*My mother's name
was Rabia Setamat*

*My father's name
was Iseu Yaristan*

My eldest sister, Sina Iseu

*The eldest brother on the
left, Farid, and eldest
sister on the right, Sina*

On the left is Samethy   *Sina and Farid*
on the right is me, Firos.
This polaroid photograph
was taken in 1979,
after our arrival at the
Khmer-Thai border.

My mother and my sister, Farida (still alive)

This was the former wooden house for the monks' residence where the Khmer Rouge used it for their accommodation. I and my friend, Thy, slept on the ground floor, and the Khmer Rouge soldiers slept on the top floor

My True History

I was born in Phnom Penh, Cambodia, in 1963. When I was four years old, I was studying at Ta Eisi Kindergarten, which was on the corner of Street 384 and Street 193. This was a preparatory school. Before the fall of Phnom Penh on 17 April 1975, my house was behind the Pakistani mosque at the corner of Street 173 and Street 384, in front of what is now Mlup Svay Restaurant 99. From the 12th to the 8th grade (equivalent to the modern 1st to the 5th), I studied at Indra Devi Primary School, next to the former Tuol Sleng High School S-21 today. Indra Tevy Primary School moved to Tuol Sleng Primary School in 1974 near the present Olympic Market. I studied at that school for a year, when I was in the eighth grade (now the fifth grade).

Both my grandfathers, paternal and maternal, were born in the Indian subcontinent in the 1880s. They were of Pashtun (Pathan) origins. Life was harsh at that time, so they left their villages as young men to look for business opportunities in other South-East Asian countries so that they could send the money back home to support their families. My paternal grandfather (Yaguistan Khan) left the Indian subcontinent in the first decade of the twentieth century. He crossed the border into Burma (Myanmar), then Thailand and he finally arrived in Cambodia. Once he was there, he set up a gemstone business in the mining town of

Pailin near the Thai-Cambodian border. A few years after his arrival, he married a local Vietnamese bride, and he had four children. My father was the youngest, with two elder sisters and one elder brother. Both his sisters left Ho Chi Minh City (Saigon), Vietnam, for Marseille, France, in 1956, two years after the French lost the Battle of Dien Bien Phu in 1954. My father stayed behind, because my mother did not want to go to France without her mother.

My maternal grandfather (Sayed Ahmad Khan) also left the Indian subcontinent, crossing the border into Burma (Myanma) and then into Laos. While he was in Laos, he married a local Laotian bride and they had four children. Like my father, my mother was the youngest. She had one elder sister and two elder brothers. With four children, my grandfather moved his family to Cambodia, and he set up a cattle business to produce fresh milk and cheese to sell to the French colonialists, because the local people did not know how to do it at that time. One of my mother's elder brothers survived the Khmer Rouge regime because he took his family, on foot, to Vietnam right after the Fall of Phnom Penh on 17 April 1975. My mother's other brother was killed by the Khmer Rouge right after they took over the government because he was a soldier in the Lon Nol republican army. Neither of my grandfathers ever once returned to their country of birth and they both passed away in Cambodia.

1: Phnom Penh

Thursday 17 April 1975 is the day that I will never forget until the day I die. That was the day the Khmer Rouge took over Phnom Penh and overthrew the government of General Lon Nol and his Republican Party. The three days before that we celebrated the traditional Khmer New Year: the 14th was a Monday, the 15th a Tuesday and the 16th a Wednesday. There were nine members in my household, including me.

On that day, at around 10 am, the Khmer Rouge took over Phnom Penh. My house at that time was near Mao Tse tung Boulevard. I left my house and headed there. When I arrived, I saw hundreds of Khmer Rouge soldiers marching in black uniforms, wearing Ho Chi Minh-style rubber shoes, donning Khmer traditional neckerchiefs (*kra ma*), and fully armed. Then I saw people coming out of their houses, standing on the street, shouting and welcoming the Khmer Rouge with great joy. Our country was at peace at last, putting a stop to all the rockets that hit the capital city almost nightly, killing thousands of people. Hopefully, the siege of the capital city had been lifted so that food supplies could come from the countryside to feed its population.

I followed the Khmer Rouge soldiers to the corner of the Bokor traffic light, at the corner of Monivong and Mao Seng Tung Boulevards. About 11:00 am, I returned home and told my parents what I had se

My father never let me borrow his red old French motorcycle; I do not know why he let me borrow it that day.

I, and my cousin, rode that motorbike to the Olympic Market and Olympic Stadium. I rode around for about an hour watching the Khmer Rouge soldiers marching eastward on Sihanouk Street. About one o'clock in the afternoon, I began to see people carrying luggage, pots, pans and other things on the street, and I asked them why. They told me that the Khmer Rouge had told them to leave their homes and leave the city for three days because US war planes were going to drop bombs on Phnom Penh. Then, I started to ride quickly my father's motorcycle back home just in case he was expecting me. The motorcycle was old, so when I rode too fast, it broke down in the middle of the road and we both had to push it all the way home.

When I arrived home, there was only my family left, and all the people in my neighbourhood had already gone. My father told me that the Khmer Rouge soldiers had come to tell him twice to leave the house to go to the countryside for three days only; there was no need for him to lock the house because the American war planes were going to bomb the city. He begged them to wait for his son to return from the market, and the Khmer Rouge soldiers even threatened him that when they came back again for the last time, if they still saw people inside the house, they would shoot to kill everybody. Luckily, I arrived home on time. My dad immediately chained his motorcycle to the column of the house, and my family hurried out of the house, missing one of my older brothers; we didn't know where he had gone. I vividly remember that, on 17 April 1975, my mother cooked goat curry and we did not even have time to eat our lunch. The Khmer Rouge soldiers drove us out of the house and we packed our goat curry and rice to eat on the street. The eight of us walked along Mao Seng Tung Boulevard, heading east toward Monivong Boulevard.

In Phnom Penh, during the time of Prince Sihanouk before he was ousted on 18 March 1970, the population was only about 600,000, but later it increased because the flames of war engulfed Cambodia. The Khmer Rouge fought with Lon Nol troops and American warplanes bombed the Khmer Rouge strongholds, destroying farmlands and houses so the people living in the provinces had to flee to Phnom Penh because they had nowhere else to go. By 17 April 1975 Phnom Penh had a population of more than two million, four times that of during the time of Prince Sihanouk.

In 1974, before the Khmer Rouge entered Phnom Penh, there were sounds of rocket shells hitting strategic military places almost every night in Phnom Penh. My house was near the Chinese embassy, and in front of it were barracks. The Khmer Rouge fired rockets at the barracks, and many rockets landed near my house. My eldest sister was hit by shrapnel, and her ankle was slightly injured. In my house, there was a trench, and every time the rockets were fired, we all had to run into it for safety.

When my family reached Mao Seng Tung Boulevard, it was already packed like sardines with evacuees, walking slowly. Sometimes we were stuck for hours. My family started walking from the Chinese embassy to the corner of the Bokor traffic light, which took us almost four hours. When my family reached the Bokor traffic light, we turned right onto Monivong Boulevard, walking towards the Monivong Bridge.

At about six o'clock in the evening, my family stopped at a villa on Monivong Blvd., which the owner had already evacuated when we arrived. We all ate our dinner and spent the night inside the villa. The next day, Friday, April 18, my family left the villa for the Monivong Bridge. When we reached an area called Kbal Thnal, just before the Monivong Bridge, we rested for another night in an abandoned house. The street was still crowded with people.

The next day, on Saturday, April 19, my family crossed the Monivong Bridge to Chbar Ampov. Inside the Chbar Ampov cinema, I saw several Lon Nol soldiers lying dead with gunshot wounds, swollen and eaten by maggots. Probably they were killed by the Khmer Rouge on 17 April.

My family continued their journey to Champuh Khaek Temple. When we arrived there, my family stopped for lunch at the shed in front of the temple.

I vividly remembered that when I was chopping the firewood with an axe for my eldest sister to cook, my left toe was cut and it bled.

2: Champuh Khaek Temple

After lunch, I and my family continued our journey, but we did not go far. We rested on the bank of the Bassac River at the southern corner of Champuh Khaek Temple to wait for the news of my brother, Farid, who hadn't returned home to join us that day on 17 April. Upon hearing the news that my brother was travelling with my aunt's family to Saang district, Koh Thom, near the Vietnamese border, my mother left to look for him and bring him back to reunite with our family at the Champuh Khaek Temple. My family rested in front of the Champuh Khaek Temple for about three nights. Every day, my brother and I rode our bicycles to look for food like papaya in Prek Pra to make soup.

On Tuesday, April 22, we heard that the French Embassy was open and would accept foreigners who wanted to leave the country. In the afternoon, my family started to pack up and left for National Road No. 1, spending the night on the road. The next day, Wednesday, April 23, my family continued our journey, in the hope of going back to Phnom Penh and entering the French Embassy. When my family reached National Road No. 1, there were two options. Hundreds of foreigners were staying at the Nirot Temple and hundreds more at the Champa Temple. In the Nirot Temple, there were many Pakistani families, including my cousin's family, who was also staying there. At that time, my father had no reason to know that this was a fatal step for him and his family. My mother wanted to turn left to the Nirot Temple, but my father did not want to go to the Nirot Temple, he instead wanted to go to the Champa Temple because he did not want to meet all the Pakistani people there. Then he led his family to the Champa Temple. This was a tragic mistake. While staying at the Champa Temple, I still saw people walking along National Road No. 1 towards Neak Leurng.

3: Champa Temple

Inside the Champa Temple's ground, there were many tall Kamping Reach (Santol) trees which were full of big fruits. I climbed them, picked their fruits and ate these whole, including the nuts because they were delicious, with a sweet and sour taste. I also took them for my family to eat. My family stayed at the Champa Temple for five nights and we heard that all the foreigners at the Nirot Temple had been taken by the Khmer Rouge to the French Embassy. As for the 400 or so foreigners at the Champa Temple, including my family, the Khmer Rouge told us the night before that we would be leaving for the French Embassy the next day. My parents told my eldest brother that when the truck arrived the next day, he had to hurry and throw our luggage on the truck, and we had to climb on the truck quickly because there were so many people. Do you know that the next day I would be an orphan for the rest of my life and that seven members of my family would die, one after another?

I learned after that in the first convoy on April 30, the Khmer Rouge transported foreigners from the French Embassy to Poipet on the Thai-Cambodian border. They travelled for three nights and four days before reaching Poipet. The Khmer Rouge were very cunning. They did not transport all of the foreigners along National Road 5 through the Chroy Changvar

Bridge. The convoys were being diverted because at that time there were still people being evacuated from the city and it was still packed on National Road 5. The foreigners were taken along National Road 4, turned right into Road Number 55, and went straight to Udong. They then re-joined National Route 5 and headed for Poipet. The French Embassy closed on May 7, and the second and last convoy left for Poipet.

Now let me go back a little bit. When my family arrived at the Champa Temple, the Khmer Rouge came to register us with other foreigners to go the French Embassy. Among them were foreigners such as Pakistanis, Indians, Taiwanese, Vietnamese, French and many others I met.

4: Return to Phnom Penh

On the morning of 29 April 1975, the Khmer Rouge lined up their trucks at the Champa temple. Foreigners were competing ferociously to board the trucks since spaces were limited. Each of the trucks was fully packed. There were about 400 foreigners including children and senior people being transported back to Phnom Penh by the Khmer Rouge. Upon arrival in Phnom Penh, the Khmer Rouge did not take us to the French Embassy. Instead, we were housed, one family per villa, along Sisowath Quay on the bank of the Tonle Sap River, and each villa was guarded by the Khmer Rouge. There were nine members in my family, including me. After lunch, my family was sitting under a tree in front of the villa, discussing why the Khmer Rouge did not take us to the French Embassy directly and they had to bring us to this villa. My older siblings, my parents, and my grandmother looked sad. Maybe they were worried about something, but we, the young ones, were not concerned at all. By dinner time, we were still waiting for the Khmer Rouge to take us to the French Embassy but they didn't come. My family had our dinner and at about 8 pm, just before going to bed, a few Khmer Rouge soldiers came into the house, where we were staying, to tell my parents, my grandmother, my 19-year-old sister and 17-year-old brother that they had to go to attend a meeting, without having to take anything with them, and the four of us children did not have to go with them and should go to bed. They said the meeting wouldn't take long and my family members would be back very soon. I asked the Khmer Rouge if I could go with my parents, but they told me not to go and stay with my three other siblings, so I agreed. I did not follow them outside the villa and did not know for sure whether my five family members went with the Khmer Rouge on foot or by car. After they were gone, the Khmer Rouge guards called in and told me to visit their house next door, for about an hour. Then I returned to sleep with my three other siblings who did not go with my parents. At about 10 pm, I still had not seen my parents, grandmother, eldest brother, and eldest sister come back home. So I went to bed. At about two o'clock in the morning, I got up to go to the toilet and still did not see them all come back home, and I went back again to sleep until 8 o'clock in the morning.

5: Chbar Ampov

When I woke up the next day, I went to ask the Khmer Rouge soldiers why my family members had not returned home. They just replied that the 'Organisation' had called them to study for a short time, and I would see them again very soon. This was the first time I heard the word 'Organisation' and I did not know who the Organisation was or what it was, but I did not ask the Khmer Rouge soldiers this question. At around 9 am on the same day, after we ate the breakfast packs that the Khmer Rouge had distributed, an American GMC military truck stopped in front of the villa where we were staying. The Khmer Rouge soldiers then told us to pack up our belongings and get into the truck. Before boarding the truck, I searched my family's belongings but did not find any of the jewellery that my mother had hidden. I knew and had seen that my parents had dozens of very valuable large Pailin gemstones, in which my father inherited from my paternal grandfather. When I got inside the truck, I was shocked because I saw all the foreign children who I had met, such as an Indian girl who was about four years old and many other French mixed-race children when we were at the Champa temple.

The Khmer Rouge transported about 70 children to work at a pig farm in Chbar Ampov. My family then had four members left. My older brother was 15 years old, I was 12 years old, my younger sister was 10 years old and my youngest brother was 8 years old. When we arrived at the pig farm, I told the Khmer Rouge soldiers that the four of us were of Pakistani Muslim descent and could not touch or eat pork. The Khmer Rouge replied that it was okay to just spray the water to wash the pigs and we did not need to touch them. The daily work there was not difficult: some children picked up pig manure, some fed the pigs, but for us, we just sprayed them with the water. When I finished work, I just went to look at the houses nearby that had been abandoned. The Khmer Rouge fed us twice a day, lunch and dinner, no breakfast. When all these pigs were ready to be slaughtered, they must have been reserved for the Khmer Rouge cadres to eat, because after three months I had never seen them distribute any pork to the people to eat.

6: Koh Krabei Village

We, and the other children, worked at the Chbar Ampov pig farm for only one week and then we were transported by the Khmer Rouge by an American military motorboat, which the Khmer Rouge had begun to use, to the village of Koh Krabei. When we and the other orphans arrived at the Koh Krabei village, we were told to go and live with the Khmer Rouge families, a few children for each family, except the four of us. We were put in the cooperative to live amongst the Khmer Rouge soldiers and I did not know why. My daily job was to distribute rice to the villagers. As for my sister, she was put to make traditional medicines with native Khmer Rouge women. At night, I and my two brothers slept in a corrugated-iron shed, while my sister was allowed to sleep with the native Khmer Rouge women. She had to sleep at their feet at night. I thought this was the biggest insult to the ' 17 April people' (that was what they called us) like us! They treated us like slaves, and we were worthless to them.

7: Champuh Khaek Village

We worked at the Koh Krabei Cooperative for about a month, and then the Khmer Rouge sent the four of us to live with two old native people named Grandmother Chea and Grandfather Thlang in the Champuh Khaek village. When we lived in the village of Champuh Khaek with the old couple, the Khmer Rouge made us cut down the bushes and planted crops. They distributed rice for us to cook for ourselves, and sometimes the old couple gave us some soup to eat with our rice. In July 1975, the Khmer Rouge announced that anyone wishing to go and live in Battambang province could register. I consulted with the old couple whether we should register to go to Battambang province or not. They replied that we should register to go. If we did not register, sooner or later, the Khmer Rouge would send us there anyway because we were not native people. The place where we lived was reserved only for the native people, and we were not allowed to live there because we were the 17 April people! The four of us then decided to register to go to live in Battambang province and we also thanked Grandma Chea and Grandpa Thlang for giving us a house to live. We boarded a boat to Battambang at Chbar Ampov with the other 17 April people.

When I was living with Grandma Chea and Grandpa Thlang, I was travelling with my friend, Thy, whom

I first met at the Champa temple. Thy's grandfather was half-French, half-Vietnamese, and Thy's mother married Thy's father, a Cambodian, a colonel in Lon Nol's army. Thy's father was missing and did not come with Thy's family. We walked from the village of Champuh Khaek to Chbar Ampov back to where I used to raise pigs about two months before. When we arrived, we did not meet the Khmer Rouge chief who was running the place. His name was Seam. We waited for him until the afternoon when he returned from a meeting in Phnom Penh. I then asked him about my parents and siblings who were summoned to the meeting. He replied that he had no news and told us not to come to his place again, and we should be careful. Luckily for us, he was still in charge, and if he hadn't been there and we had met other Khmer Rouge soldiers, we would have been in big trouble. I thanked him and we went back to the village. As for Thy's family, when they were at the Champa Temple together, there were seven members, including his grandfather, mother, older sister, Thy himself, a younger sister and two younger brothers. In 1974, his eldest brother was killed while watching a movie in a cinema in Phnom Penh when it was bombed by the Khmer Rouge. When his family was taken back to Phnom Penh, the Khmer Rouge summoned three people: Thy's eldest sister, 17 years old, mother and grandfather. By the time they arrived at the Koh Krabei village, including Thy, there were four siblings left. As for Thy's younger sister, the Khmer Rouge separated her from the others. I invited Thy and his two younger brothers to live with us with Grandma Chea and Grandpa Thlang, a few days before we departed for Battambang together, but Thy did not invite his younger sister to come with us because she was living comfortably with a Khmer Rouge family. They may have planned to marry her off with one of their sons, because she was pretty, a mix of three nationalities: French, Vietnamese and Cambodian.

8: Kampong Chhnang

In my family, there were then four siblings left. The four of us boarded the boat from Chbar Ampov at about 12 midday. The boat we were on was too crowded and there was no place to sit. The Khmer Rouge crammed us in like sardines. When we wanted to go to the toilet, it was very difficult because there was no toilet on the boat. We felt very embarrassed, and we had to do it on the edge of the boat in the open. The boat finally arrived at the port of Kampong Chhnang and docked. The people were let off the boat at about four o'clock in the morning because the boat was slow, and it had taken us nearly ten hours of travelling.

The four of us got off the boat and we all sat under a tree until about 6 am. I told my elder brother, Rashid, to look after our two younger siblings and not let them go anywhere for fear of splitting up because we only had rice, and I had to go out to ask for some fish from the villagers so that we could eat our breakfast. I left them for just over an hour to ask for fish from the villagers. They did not give it to me easily, so I went to more than 10 houses. Even though I told them that I was an orphan, they still did not give me fish because in the era of Democratic Kampuchea, no one helped anyone, everyone was looking after his/her own life. When I went to the last house, there was a family who felt sorry for me, for being an orphan. They gave me a few dried fish. I thanked them and hurried to re-join my siblings who were waiting for me under the tree.

When I arrived back at about 7 o'clock in the morning and did not see my younger sister, I asked my elder brother where she was. He replied that he did not know; she said she wanted to go out for a while and she had not come back. I told my brother to find a place to grill the fish and left to search for my sister. At around 8 am, the Khmer Rouge lined up dozens of American military GMC trucks to transport people to Pursat Province. I went to look through all the passengers on the trucks in case my sister got in there first. I walked back and forth, checking through all the trucks, and did not see my sister at all. She had simply disappeared.

At about 9 o'clock in the morning, I returned to where my brother was, while he was waiting for my sister to return, but still I had not seen her there either. We three brothers then started to eat our breakfast, which consisted of rice with grilled dried fish that my elder brother had just cooked. Soon after, the Khmer Rouge soldiers forced us to board a truck to go to Pursat Province.

9: Pursat Province

About one o'clock in the afternoon, our convoy arrived in Pursat provincial town. People were told to get off the trucks and to continue to travel by train to Battambang province. We got off our truck and I went looking for my sister again. There were thousands of people and it took me hours to search for her. I felt so exhausted, and still she could not be found. Since there were thousands of people, just to search for one person, maybe I missed her, or destiny or karma wanted to separate us: that was why I couldn't find her! I went to tell the Khmer Rouge cadre that I had lost a sister in Kampong Chhnang Province and that we could not continue our journey to Battambang province. I wanted to ask if we could wait for a few more days in case we found her again. I told the chief of the Khmer Rouge who was overseeing the evacuation and transportation of people to Battambang province that we were orphans. He then told me and my two other brothers to wait there before he contacted his superior, and he kindly allowed the three of us and Thy's family of three to stay at his place for the time being. A few days later, a Khmer Rouge VIP riding on an American military jeep with his chauffeur came to visit us. I later learned that the Khmer Rouge leader, Ros Nhim, was the secretary of the Northwest Zone. Comrade Nhim told us that there was no need for us to travel to Battambang province. We all could live and work in Pursat province.

10:   Bak Tra Mountain

The next day, the Khmer Rouge brought a car to transport my family and Thy's family, the six of us, to plant cotton at the foot of Baktra Mountain. Baktra Mountain is more than 14 kilometres from the corner of National Road 5 and Road 146 in the southwest of Pursat Provincial Town.

When we first arrived in Baktra, the Khmer Rouge let us live in a large wooden house with a high staircase with the Khmer Rouge soldiers, as well as our guardians. In 1975, Baktra Mountain had a lot of wild animals, so we had to sleep on the first floor at night because there were many wild animals walking under the house. We even saw the footprints of a tiger when we came down from the house in the morning. Sometimes the Khmer Rouge soldiers went out to hunt wild animals, such as wild boars and tigers. The tiger meat could only be salted and dried in the sun and then grilled. It could not be used to make soup because it smelled so bad. But the wild boar meat was different; the Khmer Rouge braised it with bamboo shoots since there were many bamboo trees along the canal.

I specialised in climbing coconut and other trees because in my house in Phnom Penh, we had two tall areca palm trees, two coconut trees, a jujube tree, a milk fruit tree, a mango tree, a pomegranate tree, a jackfruit tree, two wax apple trees, a gooseberry tree, a bilimbi tree and so on. So I used to climb up the two tall areca palm trees to pick their fruits for my grandmother when they were ripe. My grandmother used to chew them daily: betel leaves mixed with lime and areca nuts.

When I was growing cotton at the foot of Baktra Mountain, my friend, Thy, and I always went to abandoned houses to pick coconuts. One day, I climbed a coconut tree, we ate some at the site and brought back home two coconuts. A kind Khmer Rouge soldier told me to throw them away so that other soldiers would not see me holding onto them, so I took the coconuts to the bush and threw them away and thanked him for that because I didn't know that we were not allowed to pick them. Comrade Ros Nhim, Secretary of the Northwest Zone, planned to open a large orphanage at the foot of Baktra Mountain. Every day I saw the Khmer Rouge soldiers transporting orphans in trucks to my place of residence. By August 1975, the number of orphans had risen to hundreds.

The work of growing cotton was not very hard, but I was tired of work, tired of living with hundreds of other children, and tired of working without a day off. I also heard from other senior 17 April people (new people in contrast to the Khmer Rouge native people who were members of the Communist Party of Kampuchea) like me said that if I wanted to escape to Thailand, I should escape through the Five-Tamarind-Tree Pass, Battambang province. I was born and raised in Phnom Penh and at my young age, I did not know the geography of Battambang and Pursat provinces at all. I just knew that Battambang province shares the border with Thailand, especially Pailin town, because in the Lon Nol era, I heard Sin Sisamouth singing the songs about Pailin which is adjacent to the Cambodian-Thai border, and I knew that Thailand was a free country, not a communist country like Cambodia.

I had a big goal! I wanted to go to Battambang Province and escape to Thailand for my freedom and my future. Does anyone want to work without pay, work seven days a week without a day off, without schooling, without markets to go to, without temples to worship, without western medicines to cure you when you are sick? Why should we let the Khmer Rouge's children rule and torment us, kill their own people, especially as they considered us 17 April people as free slaves? What should I do when I was only 12 years old, had no experience in life at all and especially without parents to take care of me? My youngest brother was just eight years old, a complete burden on me. As for my older brother, he was 15 years old, but he did not care about his younger siblings at all, he only thought about himself. About a month after living in this orphanage, my elder brother, Rashid, ran away and he did not tell me beforehand at all. The Khmer Rouge soldiers arrested him and they severely tortured him. His face was swollen badly and bleeding all over and he looked unrecognisable. After he was tortured, he was tied up under an orange tree for other orphans to see so they would not imitate him. At that time, the Khmer Rouge soldiers who were running the orphanage did not have the right to kill orphans on the spot unless they sought for permission from their Khmer Rouge leaders, such as Comrade Ros Nhim. A few days after being tortured, my elder brother escaped again and he remains missing until today. The Khmer Rouge soldiers did not tell me directly, but they told other orphans that the tiger had already eaten my brother. If this was true or false, I could not say, but I knew that he disappeared when he ran away the second time and did not return.

If I could have read the map like today, I would not have wanted to escape to Thailand through Battambang Province, but to go west because Pursat province is also adjacent to Thailand. It is only about 160 kilometres to Trat Province, Thailand! At that time, I did not know the geography at all. If I wanted to escape, I thought, I would just escape along National Road 5 to Battambang Province.

One night I was discussing with another orphan sleeping next to me that I wanted to eat some coconuts and I had mastered the art of climbing coconut trees or any kinds of trees. Then he and I made a rendezvous after lunch the next day. We would go to pick some coconuts after lunch. Once we were there, I told him to wait under the coconut tree to keep watch for and alert me if anyone approaching our area. I stared to climb to the top of the coconut tree, picked and dropped about five to six coconuts. Suddenly, I heard the footsteps of someone approaching, I then looked down and saw a Khmer Rouge soldier holding an AK47 Assault Rifle gun, waiting for me under the coconut tree that I was on. I also saw that orphan, my collaborator, who should have been keeping an eye out for me but hadn't alerted me at all. I was wondering how come the Khmer Rouge knew about this! In fact, that orphan who was supposed to steal the coconuts with me had already reported our plan to the Khmer Rouge the night before. The Khmer Rouge soldier threatened to shoot me if I didn't come down immediately. I believed that he would have shot me if he could. When I got back to the ground, he beat, and tortured me with the butt of his gun, and shouted at me:

"You bloody enemy of the Party, you betrayer of the Organisation! Don't we give you enough food to eat and you still keep on stealing coconuts without asking us for permission!"

He kept on hitting my head, my face, my body, and I was bleeding profusely. It felt very painful at first, but after a while, my body became numb and I almost didn't feel any pain at all. The Khmer Rouge soldier did not kill me; he would have shot me on the spot if he could, but if he wanted to kill an orphan, he would have to get permission from the high-ranking cadre running the orphanage there.

After I was tortured, I was tied up under an orange tree, the same process as my elder brother after he was caught for escaping from the orphanage, to set an example or to scare other orphans not to do such thing. At that time, my youngest brother, Fuad, also came to look at me being tied up. He had a sad look on his face and but he did not say anything. This was the first experience in my 12-year-old life that convinced me not to trust anyone else if I wanted to survive the regime.

From April 1975 to August 1975, of my nine family members, there were then only two siblings left, me and my youngest brother. As for my friend, Thy, and his family, they went from seven members to three members left: he himself and his two younger brothers. Thy had two younger brothers. One was 10 years old and the other was 8 years old, the same age as my younger brother.

One night, about a week after I was tortured, I consulted with Thy about my plan to escape from this orphanage to Battambang Province then to Thailand for our freedom. We both decided to escape back to Pursat train station because at that time the Khmer Rouge were still evacuating people by train to Battambang Province.

11: Stung Touch Village

One night, the five of us set off on foot on Route 156 toward National Road 5. If we measure the distance now, it is 13.4 km from the foot of Bak Tra Mountain to Stung Touch village, which is next to the railway tracks. At that time, I could walk four kilometres per hour. If I walked alone, it would have a maximum of four hours. But then the six of us left about an hour past midnight, walking and stopping because there were three small children among us and we all felt scared of tigers and other wild animals. We only heard the cries of wild animals in the forest, and the three younger children were more terrified than us. We were also carrying our belongings. I used a salt bag as my suitcase and my little brother carried a steel kettle. Our journey was delayed when we reached Stung Touch village. We saw people planting rice in the fields near the road that we travelled along. They all turned their faces and looked at the six of us. We were scared of being captured by the Khmer Rouge so we walked through the rice fields instead of on the road, trying to make a detour. When we reached Stung Touch village, about 200 metres from the railway, the Khmer Rouge soldiers stopped all of us and asked where we came from and where we were going. I told the Khmer Rouge soldiers that the five of us intended to travel to Battambang to look for our parents and siblings who we had been separated from since 17 April 1975. The Khmer Rouge also saw us walking from south to north, towards the provincial town of Pursat. I told them that we had left the Baktra orphanage and they asked us if we had sought permission from the cadre who were running the orphanage. I replied that we had applied for travel documents but they had not been issued. The Khmer Rouge did not believe me, and then they locked up the five of us in a room on the ground floor of the house where the Khmer Rouge soldiers were residing. They also provided us with rice and some fish to eat for lunch and dinner, no breakfast. The next day, I asked the Khmer Rouge soldiers again if they could allow us to travel by train to Battambang Province, and they replied that they had contacted the cadre running the orphanage where we came from and all the five of us had to be sent back to the orphanage. This meant that we had travelled through the forest, with the fear of being killed by wild animals, in vain!

My friend, Thy, and I also discussed what to do next: whether they would send all of us back to the orphanage or whether we could run away to get on the train. What should we do with the three children? In the end, the two of us decided to run away and leave the children behind in the cell.

Why did I run away and leave my youngest brother, who was only eight years old at the time? I still feel very guilty up until now every time I think about it, even though it happened more than 45 years ago. Whenever I think about my escape, I always feel that I had made a serious mistake, because he was my responsibility. I didn't bring him along with me and I didn't take care of him properly! My 12-year-old brain at the time thought that it would be better to leave him in the cell where he would have shelter and food and would survive. I did not know the lay of the land; where I was going would be a big risk for him, and where would I get the food to feed him? One might have known that during the Pol Pot's regime, money was not used at all, hence no markets. We all had to eat communally, work for them for free, seven days a week; all schools were closed, and we all were treated like free slaves. Finally, I decided not to let him go on an adventure with me because I saw firsthand that when we ran away from the orphanage, the three children had a very hard time. They felt tired and hungry and did not sleep through the night, they were in fear and walked for tens of kilometres at a slow pace. What about you? If you were me, what would you have done in this situation? Just assume that you are a 12-year-old orphaned boy and you have an 8-year-old younger brother in your care without any means of support.

12: Okreat Village

Before I made an escape through the window, I looked at my poor little brother, who was sleeping so soundly, and I said goodbye to him in my heart that we would meet again one day when our country became free of the communist dictatorship. As for Thy's two younger brothers, they were also sleeping soundly. The Khmer Rouge soldiers did not put handcuffs or iron shackles on us, they just locked us from the outside. We both escaped through the wooden window by breaking it at about two o'clock in the morning. We hid ourselves in the bush near the railway tracks until dawn.

A train with very long railway carriages for transporting cattle, left over from the French colonial times, was parked north of Stung Touch village, southeast of Pursat Provincial town. At about eight o'clock in the morning, I saw people boarding the train, and we both got out of the bush and jumped into the cattle train: no seats at all in them. We both sat quietly at the corner of the carriage. Our heads were covered with Krama (Cambodian traditional clothes); only our faces were showing. After a while, I saw the Khmer Rouge soldiers I knew, checking or looking for escapees on the train. They were the ones who arrested us, including the three children. If you have faith in a religion, there is a Cambodian saying: មាហ់ហាំង ជញ្ជាំងបិទ, roughly translated into English as "closing the wall", which means that the person has been transformed so that one cannot see his/her face or think that he/she is someone else with the help of a higher being. Either that, or the Khmer Rouge soldiers took pity on us or didn't want to kill us and let us run away, because we looked at each other. They saw our faces, and we saw their faces, and they just walked away from the train's carriage where we both were sitting. To this day, I still do not understand that event that happened more than forty years ago. And what do you think of it?

The distance from Pursat Provincial Town to Okreat village is more than 50 kilometres before Mong Russey railway station. Travelling by train took us approximately four hours. The train left at around 9 am and arrived at Okreat train station at about one o'clock in the afternoon, because the train stopped many times and it was running very slowly.

The passengers that were on the train with me were Cambodians of Chinese descent who used to live in cities and towns more than ethnic Cambodians. When the train stopped at the Okreat train station, the Khmer Rouge soldiers ordered all the passengers to get off. The city-dweller Chinese people, once they got off the train, started to trample on the rice seedlings that the Khmer Rouge had planted, because they thought that they were either weeds or grass. They couldn't tell the difference. The Khmer Rouge, wielding bamboo sticks, chased and beat our Chinese brothers and sisters and they ran all over the fields.

I was not beaten with sticks because I knew exactly what the rice seedlings were and what the weeds or grass were.

Dozens of ox carts were lining up to transport the train passengers to resettle in villages and communes designated by the Organisation. My friend, Thy and I, did not hop on the ox cart with them. I went straight to see the Khmer Rouge cadre who were supervising the transportation of people to the communes and villages there and said, "Comrade elder brother!" (I was the one who spoke because Thy did not know how speak, as he came from a high society or cultured class and never got involved with the poor people). "We have been separated from our parents and siblings since we left Phnom Penh. Can we both travel further to look for them, just in case we see them?"

They replied, "The Organisation does not allow anyone to move forward or to look for any lost relatives. Stay where you are allocated and start working, and do not worry at all about your parents or siblings, the Organisation will take care of them all". Then they took us to live temporarily in a house near the railway tracks.

In the next morning, the Khmer Rouge soldiers distributed a light hoe to each one of us to uproot the grass in the vegetable garden patches because the Organisation did not want anyone being idle. The work itself was not hard and we were given enough rice to eat, even though it was not nutritious, but I was very tired of living under the Khmer Rouge regime and I didn't want to be stuck in this godforsaken place. I still wanted to flee to Thailand for my future and freedom, if it was possible.

Once, as I was weeding, the hoe hit my left ankle and I had a small cut. I did not pay much attention to it for the first few days, but then it became infected because my feet were dirty and wet every day while I was working. The wound slowly increased in size. I had to treat it myself and it never healed. The Khmer Rouge either had no Western medicine or did not wish to give it to the people on April 17. I heard from other people that my wound could be cured with tamarind leaves. So, I went to pick a lot of tamarind leaves, boiled them and used the sour water from the leaves to wash my wound a few times a day during work breaks so that I could get rid of the pus. After washing it, I wrapped a strip of cloth around my infected wound so that, I believed, it could heal faster.

As the days passed by, the wound started to hurt me terribly, and I kept on using the sour water from the tamarind leaves. It helped me a bit but not much because it became wet every day with dirty water. When the wound became severely infected, it became very deep, and I could actually see the bone of my ankle. I kept on telling the Khmer Rouge about it, but they completely ignored me and ordered me to keep on working. They never gave me a day off, probably because they thought that my wound was insignificant.

Do you know that I had to treat this wound all by myself for more than a year until it completely healed, and that I bear the scar of my wound to this day? This is a good souvenir from the Great Democratic Kampuchea, the Great Leap Forward of Pol Pot, Ieng Sary, Khieu Thirith and Khieu Ponnary! Did you know that Ieng Sary's son was still studying abroad, enjoying good food, good life and good education whilst the people of Cambodia were starving to death for three years, eight months and twenty days?

13: Prek Chik

Thy and I both lived and worked with the Khmer Rouge for two weeks and then were sent to the Prek Chik orphanage. We both ran away from the Baktra orphanage and then we got trapped in another orphanage! Prek Chik's orphanage was about 17km by a shortcut to the southwest of Okreat village. The orphanage had four to five hundred boys and girls in a very crowded environment, living under strict rules. We had to get up at 5 o'clock in the morning, attend the meeting, listen to the speeches about the Khmer Rouge Organisation, sing revolutionary songs and criticise each other and autocriticise before going to work in the rice fields. They did not give us breakfast and our stomachs were empty in the morning. At 11 o'clock in the morning, we had our first break and walked back to the communal canteen for lunch. At 12 o'clock midday, we had to leave for work until 5 pm before returning to our accommodation. The work there itself was not so difficult or heavy. It was similar to the work at the Baktra orphanage, but I hated the routines and living with hundreds of other children.

We both stayed at the Prek Chik orphanage for about three nights and then we ran away again. We escaped at around 12 midnight because there were no Khmer Rouge soldiers guarding the orphanage. Perhaps they thought that we were the most easily controlled and pliable children and would not revolt. We walked non-stop, heading north toward Okreat village. When we got to the railway tracks near the Okreat train station, we stopped and hid ourselves in the bushes near there to relax after a long walk with an empty stomach. At around 9 am, we started to walk westerly toward Maung Russey and at about 10 am we reached the Dontry River. We did not walk across the steel railway bridge because we thought that it would be guarded by the Khmer Rouge soldiers, so we walked back to National Road 5. When we reached National Road 5, we continued to walk towards the town of Maung Russey district. When we arrived at Maung Russey, both of us were stopped and asked by the Khmer Rouge soldiers where we were heading. During the working hours, the Khmer Rouge did not allow people to walk around freely, and everyone had to work, including the children. I informed the Khmer Rouge soldiers that we were both searching for our parents and siblings and we had been separated since April, but we did not have any travel permits. I did not tell the Khmer Rouge soldiers that we had run away from the Prek Chik orphanage. About an hour later, two Khmer Rouge soldiers, armed with AK47 Assault Rifles, escorted us both to the village of Kon Khaek, about five kilometres along the Dontry River.

14:   Koun Khaek Village

Once we arrived at Kon Khaek, we were handed over to the cooperative committee in front of Ek Sovann Temple, also called Kon Khaek Temple. They then took us to sit in the communal canteen and we were asked why we were travelling without travel documents. I also told the cooperative committee that I had been separated with my parents and other siblings when I had to leave Phnom Penh and was now looking for them. This was my usual strategy whenever I was arrested during Pol Pot's Democratic Kampuchea. The official interrogating us did not say anything and he spoke to us both with compassion. As far as I could see, not all the Khmer Rouge were evil at that time. Some of them were really good and compassionate. He also told us that we did not need to go anywhere and we could work on the farm in his cooperative.

As I was eating my lunch, I suddenly saw a young and beautiful mixed-race lady with long brown hair, white skin and a French-looking appearance, standing by the window outside the canteen. I just looked at her for a moment and I thought that she was my eldest sister, because she had a similar height, hair colour and facial features but her voice was different and then I realised that she wasn't my sister at all.

In that evening I went up to the house of the French-looking lady where she was living. I saw a bed, pillow, blanket and mosquito net, as if she had the same rights as the Khmer Rouge native people. I was wondering why she had such privileges because she slept on a bed with a real blanket, pillow and mosquito net! Right after 17 April 1975, until then, I never had the luxury of sleeping with a pillow, a blanket, and a mosquito net. Sometimes, I used a rice sack made of hemp material as a blanket on a cold night and it made me itchy all over but at least it kept me warm. The young lady was named Phal. She was about 20 years old, very slender and the most beautiful lady in the village. I also asked her background and how she drifted to live in this godforsaken village. She told me that she had reached the Khmer-Thai border in Poipet and was about to cross the bridge into Thailand with other foreigners, and suddenly, she was stopped by a high-ranking Khmer Rouge chief. That Khmer Rouge chief brought her here to live in this village in order to be his future wife.

Sister Phal asked me about my background and about my name and I told her that my name was Firos, and my friend's name was Sola Samethy. He was of French, Vietnamese and Khmer heritage. She then said to us, "You two should stop using all those names and instead you should use real Khmer names such as Friday (សុក្រ) or Saturday (សៅរ៍) because the Khmer Rouge are racists and they do not like people using foreign-sounding names."

The Khmer Rouge were themselves hypocrites.

They did not like foreigners, but they won the war by relying on other nations for their armaments and aid, especially Communist China! I then took her advice and chose the name "Saturday" until the day of liberation on 7 January 1979.

Sister Phal was very kind to me. She always gave me advice on how to adapt or change my behaviour living under the Khmer Rouge regime if I wanted to survive. I should be flexible, work hard, and obedient to the Organisation. She even let me sleep on her bed! She saw that I had only one change of clothes, so she gave me one of her T-shirts, brought over from Phnom Penh. I thanked her and used it until 1977, when it was worn out and torn apart!

Let me tell you a story about Sister Phal from approximately four years later. In June 1979, I was travelling from Battambang to Phnom Penh. I stopped at Mong Russey and walked to this same village of Kon Khaek, where I had lived four years before. I went there out of curiosity, not knowing if Sister Phal was alive or dead or if she had moved out. When I arrived at edge of Kon Khaek village, I asked the villagers if they knew a woman who was of French descent named Phal. In June 1975 during the Khmer Rouge regime, she used to live in this village and one man told me that he did not know the name of the woman called Phal, but he knew a woman of mixed race who had a baby. She was called Mother of Ty. Suddenly, I felt that it had to be her because there was no mixed- race person in this faraway village except Sister Phal! Then I asked him about the location of Mother of Ty's house. Once I got to that location, I looked under a tiled-roof wooden house and saw a lady holding a baby girl in her arms. We looked at each other for a moment, and then I realised that she was my Sister Phal indeed! After only four years, her beauty had diminished. I asked her, "Where is the father of your daughter?" She replied that her husband had gone to attend a meeting in Battambang Provincial Town. She narrated that the Khmer Rouge had forced her to get married; if she had not got married, she would have been executed. And her current husband was the same Khmer Rouge chief who had brought her from the Cambodian-Thai border in 1975.

When Cambodia was liberated from the Pol Pot regime on 7 January 1979, her husband started to work with the new government again and became a district chief and had his own motorbike to ride to attend a meeting in Battambang Provincial Town.

I slept at her house for one night, ate dinner with steamed Cambodian traditional fermented fish called "prahok" with rice which was prepared by her. It was delicious, because I knew that she was very poor and this showed her kindness towards me.

During that night, while I was sleeping at her house, the Khmer Rouge entered her village, they fired gun-shots, and made me feel terrified all over again. The next day, I asked her and to bring daughter to run away to Phnom Penh with me, which meant that she ran away from her ex-Khmer Rouge husband. She replied, "I cannot run away from my daughter's father and I want my daughter to have a father to call and to be looked after." I believed that was her destiny and her daughter had to have a father. I understood her feelings, I said goodbye to her and have not seen her again till this day. Now let me go back to my story again.

15: ODambang Village

Thy and I stayed at the Koun Khaek village for about three weeks and then we escaped again during the night, back to the Mong Russey Town. When I ran away from her village, I did not tell Sister Phal at all. I was afraid that I would be emotional, or I was afraid that she would stop me from running away, because if we did not know the geography of the land, we did not have any travel permit and it would be very difficult for us to survive travelling without food on the road.

At that time, I did not feel scared of death at all, but before I died, I had to use my intellect and my 12-year-old brain on my own first. This time, we both walked on the train tracks. We did not dare to walk on National Road 5, and we did not want to walk fast. As we approached each train station, we had to bypass through the rice-fields for fear of being caught by the Khmer Rouge soldiers guarding the stations.

To the west of Moung Russey Town, there was a village called Kouk Trom. It was a brand new village and I saw all the Cambodian-Chinese people who had been evacuated by the Khmer Rouge from other provinces. They had settled there in almost their thousands and lived in that overcrowded village. Why do I mention this village? Because a year later, when I re-entered the village of Kouk Trom, most of the Cambodian-Chinese people had been wiped out and there were only about seventy children and their mothers left. The Cambodian-Chinese had nothing to eat at all and they only ate tree leaves and grass like animals. The Khmer Rouge did not care about them at all. They just let them die like animals. When there were too many deaths, the Khmer Rouge no longer let them work, they just let them find anything they could find to eat, because that brand new village had nothing at all to eat. Who would had thought that our country should fall to such a situation?

Thy and I slept without food for two nights, walked on the train tracks the entire journey, drank water only in the rice fields. The next day, we travelled through Thepdey Mountain (also called Tapde Mountain). The distance from the Kon Khaek village to the ODambang village is only about 50km. We had to travel for more than two days because we walked through many rice fields and had to bypass all the train stations because most of the train stations were guarded by the Khmer Rouge soldiers.

When we arrived at the ODambang village at about 8 am, we searched in a field near the railway lines to look for something to eat and we came across a pineapple orchard. I broke a large and ripe pineapple from its stem with my hands because I did not have a knife. I used my teeth to peel the pineapple skin and its sharp thorns pierced my gums and it bled, but I did not feel any pain at all because I had not eaten for more than two days and I was famished. I ate the whole pineapple and then I started to feel nauseous. I sat down for a while and then I started vomiting. While I was vomiting loudly, I suddenly saw the Khmer Rouge soldiers with AK-47 rifles approaching us. They asked us where we came from, why we were not working and came to steal pineapples in his orchard. I replied to the Khmer Rouge soldiers that we had been travelling without food for a few days then and we were very hungry. So we ate his pineapples one each without asking for their permission and we were sorry.

I used the same strategy again by telling them that we both were looking for our parents and siblings because we were separated more than four months ago since we left Phnom Penh. The Khmer Rouge soldiers took pity on both of us and escorted us to their residence. When we arrived at their house, they let us eat rice with delicious braised fish at our own leisure. We both ate so much because we had not eaten for more than two days.

At around 12 noon, the Khmer Rouge soldiers took us both to live with the ODambang Village Cooperative Committee. It was like taking me to live in paradise! The two cooperative heads, a married couple without children, were both in their late 40s. I called them Father and Mother and they both loved me like their child. They did not let us eat communally with the other 'new' people (the 17 April people). They let the two of us eat and live in their house with them. They were very kind and took pity on us. I believed that not all the Khmer Rouge were bad after all. I had often seen really nasty cooperatives.

I lived with my newly-adopted Khmer Rouge parents for about a week, then my adopted father sent my friend, Thy, to work, sleep and eat in the mobile unit far away from home. He let me live with him because, I guessed, he loved me more than Thy. I really knew how to please and pamper him. Sometimes, I gave him a full-body massage because I used to do it for my grandmother, back home in Phnom Penh. My daily job was just to go fishing a little bit. I lived comfortably, ate well, and did not want to run away again because I had been struggling for months to survive!

I lived with my adopted parents for about a month, then out of nowhere, I saw my friend, Thy, who had come back to visit us from the mobile unit. He was thin from lack of food, sleep and overwork. He was not healthy like me, because I ate well with my adopted parents. In every meal, we had at least two to three courses of food. There were grilled fish, pickles, stir-fry vegetables with real meat and sometimes beef jerky. I lived with them like living in heaven, if I compared my then life with the lives of the 17 April (new) people. My newly adopted parents were the Khmer Rouge native people. They got to eat delicious and healthy food because they struggled and fought against the Lon Nol and the American governments for a long time and they were victorious.

During that night, my friend, Thy, whispered to

me that we had to escape from this place to go to the Battambang Provincial Town and then travel to Thailand through the 5-Tamarind-Tree-Pass. I had often heard from the senior new people that this pass was the easiest and shortest way to reach the Thai-Cambodian border. I angrily replied to Thy, "You go alone, because I live here comfortably, eat well, sleep well, have enough food to eat and work less, and I do not have to work as hard as others."

My friend listened to me and probably felt overwhelmed. He begged me that he could not travel alone, that we had been together since the Baktra Orphanage in Pursat Province. Since I ate well, slept well, had I forgotten the hardships and memories between the two of us? What! I didn't to reply to him immediately and started to roll a cigarette with a Sangke tree leave, since there were no tobacco papers available at that time. During that time I knew how to smoke already because my own parents were assumed dead and could not come to rebuke me for smoking. I smoked and thought for a long time and started to feel sorry for my friend. I thought that I should not abandon him, even though I ate well and slept well and we shared the good and bad times together. I knew for sure that when I escaped from this comfortable place, I would face the same hardship and starvation as before. So what could I do? Be happy alone? Finally, I decided to escape with my friend that night.

My adopted father provided for me and my friend

black shirts, black pants, green caps, and Ho Chi Minh rubber-tyre shoes (complete uniforms of the Khmer Rouge). We both wore these clothes, very proudly, like the children of the Khmer Rouge cadre.

16: Battambang Municipal Cadastral Survey Prison

We both ran away from the ODambang village at about three o'clock in the morning. We walked along the train tracks. As we approached the town, we hid in an abandoned house by the train tracks until the late afternoon, then we set off again. We had discussed between ourselves that we would have to enter the town of Battambang that night. As we were approaching the Sangke River's steel railway bridge, we stopped and thought for a moment what to do. We had two options. Either we would walk across the railway bridge or swim across the river. I was good at swimming because I once nearly drowned in a deep-water diving pool at the Olympic Stadium in Phnom Penh.

Let me tell you the story of my drowning. In 1974, I scaled the fence and jumped into the Olympic Stadium swimming pool section because I did not have the money to buy a ticket and the fence was near the pool. When I arrived there, I saw the divers swimming and floating in the pool. The water in the pool was an attractive blue. I thought that it was shallow, and so I jumped straight into the pool. I was submerged because the water was too deep and my feet couldn't touch the bottom of the pool. This pool was for deep diving, not shallow: there were two pools, one shallow and one deep, but I picked the wrong one. When I was drowning, I tried to kick my legs hard. My nose then emerged from the water and then I submerged again. The divers swimming next to me just ignored me because they thought I could swim. I felt like I might be drowning and dying then, because no one helped me, but my fate did not allow me to die at that time. And then I started panicking and kicked my legs so hard that I drifted to the edge of the pool and clung to it. I felt as if I was being born again. From the day that I was nearly drowned, I was determined to learn how to swim. I often went to practise swimming in the Mekong River, in front of the royal palace, and the dirty water pond just outside the Olympic Stadium, because from time to time the used pool water was drained outside the stadium. It was just like an artificial lake for storing dirty water at that time.

My friend, Thy, was not as good at swimming as I was. At that time the rainy season had begun and the water was almost bursting banks of the Sangke River. We both watched from a distance and saw two Khmer Rouge soldiers guarding the end of the railway bridge. Coincidentally, at that time, I saw dozens of Khmer Rouge children marching across the railway bridge to the west. Thy and I sneaked into the last row and started to march with them. Maybe they were returning to their homes after work, because it was about five o'clock in the afternoon. The two soldiers guarding the railway bridge did not notice us, as we were dressed in black, wearing green Khmer Rouge caps, and the Ho Chi Minh rubber shoes, which my Khmer Rouge adoptive father had given us. When we reached the west bank of the river, we both left the ranks of children and hid in an uninhabited house, because in Battambang as well as in Phnom Penh, the Khmer Rouge had evacuated all the people to work on the farms in the countryside.

During the first night in Battambang Provincial Town, we both slept without food. We didn't know where and how to find food because we entered the town illegally and we didn't dare to go to the Khmer Rouge houses to beg for food in case we got caught.

In the next morning, we went to look for something edible in abandoned houses and we found only soy sauce and fish sauce but no rice! We picked papayas; some were ripe, some were still green, and when we ate a lot of them we felt full.

In the evening, we walked all over Battambang Provincial Town and we reached the Battambang train station. Nearby, there was a hotel full of Chinese communist experts or advisors from the Communist China (they were friends of the Pol Pot government), and in front of the hotel there was a cafeteria reserved exclusively for Chinese advisors. As we both walked pass the cafeteria, we saw the Chinese advisors eating delicious food and the smell of cooking wafted the air, making our stomachs rumble. We did not dare to go inside the cafeteria to ask for food because we were afraid that the Khmer Rouge would arrest us and so we went back to our hiding place to sleep without food again on Street Number 1 along the Sangke River.

On the third day, we walked up and down the town and we saw the road sign to Pailin Town, which is situated near the Cambodian-Thai border. We were very happy because we found our way to the Thai border, but we did not dare to walk on that road yet. We intended to wait for a while because we were starving and we needed to find food to eat fast so that we would have the energy to travel to Thailand for our freedom. Then we went back to sleep in our hiding place.

For three days we did not have a single grain of rice in our stomachs. We ate only different types of fruits that we could find and drank water in the Sangke River.

During the third night, I was so exhausted and felt very hungry. So I fell asleep fast after the sunset. While I was sleeping and dreaming of food, I heard someone was trying to wake me up. But this was not a dream, it was a reality. I suddenly woke up and felt numb all over my body. I was wondering how the Khmer Rouge soldiers knew where I was hiding, because there were thousands of empty houses in Battambang Town which had been evacuated by the Khmer Rouge. The evacuees had been farming in the countryside since April 1975 and only later I did realise that it was none other than my best friend, Thy, who had brought the Khmer Rouge soldiers to arrest me. When I fell asleep, he went to ask for food at the Khmer Rouge's cafeteria that cooked for Chinese advisors/experts and then he was arrested. He told the Khmer Rouge soldiers that there was a friend of his who was sleeping, hungry, and thirsty. So he brought them to our hiding spot to arrest me. I guessed my friend did not want to be separated from me or he did not want to be arrested alone.

My plan to flee to Thailand had been thwarted again because of Thy's impatience and foolishness. He should have waited for the cafeteria to close and tried to break inside it to search for food. Instead, he went inside the cafeteria to ask the Khmer Rouge for food, but still he was not allowed to eat, and he was imprisoned for another night without food. I believed this was my friend's ignorance and stupidity.

I missed my adopted Khmer Rouge parents in ODambang village very much. I was living comfortably with them, I ate delicious food, and I slept well. I should not have felt sorry for my friend and decided to run away from this comfortable place, and maybe my destiny was written!

17: Battambang Provincial Town, September 1975

We were both tied up by the Khmer Rouge soldiers and were escorted to prison at the old municipal cadastral survey site with its building dating back to the French colonial era, on the banks of the Sangke River, on Street Number 1, near the Battambang Provincial Museum. Now the building had been demolished. Prisoners there were not shackled. Most of them travelled without travel documents issued by their village, commune and district chiefs. During that time, village, commune, and district chiefs could not easily issue travel documents to the 17 April/new people to travel at will. They were forced to work on the farms to increase rice production. This was the policy of the Khmer Rouge Revolutionary Organisation.

I was the youngest of all the prisoners and was just 12 years old at that time. There were more than 100 prisoners crammed inside the building. Every day the Khmer Rouge soldiers escorted the prisoners to work disassembling abandoned houses and distributing them to the villages. The food the Khmer Rouge provided for the prisoners was appalling. They did not give us rice to eat at all. We ate only watery rice porridge with sour soup, using banana trunks as vegetables; no meat, hence no nutrients at all. They just put a little bit of salt, fermented fish and that was it.

Ever since I was born, I had never heard or seen anyone eating rice porridge with banana trunk sour soup. Only the great Democratic Kampuchea, led by the idiots who received the scholarships to study in France! If we could work on the rice farms, we could find crabs, snails, mice/rats or fish to eat to increase our energy and then our work production and also to strengthen our immune system against diseases. But if we were trapped in this building, we could not find anything to supplement our tasteless meals.

Living in this prison, my health began to decline gradually because I could only eat watery rice porridge with salt. I could not eat sour soup with banana trunks. The Sangke River was just next to the old Ministry of Cadastral Survey building, and it was teeming with fish. If the Khmer Rouge had just sent one or two prisoners to fish in the river for food, our food would be tasty and full of nutrients. But they did not do that. At that time, I was only 12 years old. I was separated from my parents and siblings and there was no one to take care of me except the Khmer Rouge Organisation. I didn't know why they tortured us, the 17 April/ new people.

After more than two weeks in this prison, my health deteriorated. I ate liquid rice porridge with salt only, and I was very angry with my friend, Thy. Firstly, he asked me to run away from the ODambang village, where I had enough to eat and I lived comfortably with my adopted Khmer Rouge parents. Secondly,

he went to ask for food, was arrested and brought Khmer Rouge soldiers to arrest me again. What h done could not be undone! I did not talk much wit my friend since I had been in this prison. I began to have a fever, and my body was emaciated. I became dizzy when I got up from bed and was unable to walk.

In this prison, sick people who did not go to work were detained by the Khmer Rouge and locked inside. The building had two floors. One morning, I had a bad fever. My body temperature was so hot that I started to hallucinate. The Khmer Rouge did not give me any medicines, they only gave me some Khmer traditional herbal medicines called "rabbit's poo". I began to feel suffocated in this building because all the windows were closed and sealed from the outside, no fresh air coming in. I thought that I was dying and I started to run downstairs and once I reached the door, I started to kick, knock and bang hard on the locked door. I really don't know where I got the energy from. The Khmer Rouge shouted from the outside, "Why are you knocking on the door, and what is your problem?" I did not answer their questions, I only kept knocking and knocking. After a while, the Khmer Rouge started to open the door, holding a big stick, maybe a solid bamboo stick and was about to hit my head with it, and somehow when he saw me, probably because I was small, skinny and vulnerable, he didn't hit me. He dropped the stick and I took this opportunity and quickly ran across the road to get away from this

horrible prison as far as possible. A few Khmer Rouge soldiers chased after me and when they caught me, they touched my body and they realised that I had a high temperature and was hallucinating. They carried me back to the prison building, pushed me inside and locked the door. I received no medicines from them at all and they were just going to let me die in that building.

About a few days later, miraculously, I recovered from my fever, but I was still very weak. I said to the Khmer Rouge chief who was running the prison there, "Elder brother comrade, I cannot eat rice porridge, I would like to eat rice. Can you give me some rice to cook?"

He replied, "No, we have to eat equally. The other prisoners are eating porridge, why do you alone want to eat rice?"

I used a new strategy and said to him, "Elder brother comrade, I know how to do a massage, you can let me to try it, because I used to do it for my grandmother. I am very skilful. I know how to roll the skin on your back (swinging technique), pull your ears, arms and hair, rubbing your temples and twist your neck."

The Khmer Rouge chief then let me try to give him a full body massage. After I had given him the massage, he said that he felt relieved. Then he gave me half a can of rice to cook and a few dried fish. The dried fish was reserved for the Khmer Rouge only. They only ate solid rice with nutritious food, not watery rice

porridge like us. He then told me to eat quietly, and should not let others know that he gave me the food. I believed that he was compassionate and took pity on me, since I was the smallest and the youngest amongst all the other prisoners.

Let me tell you another story about my effective massage, but we have to fast-forward seven years. In 1982, I was a refugee in Malaysia on an island called Pulau Bidong. It was the United Nations refugee camp which housed thousands of Vietnamese who travelled by boat to Malaysia. I got to know and often talked to the UN chief on the island. His name was John Singh. He was big and tall; his height was about 1.9 metres. He told me that he had a very sore back, in the shoulder blade area. He had been suffering for almost a week and it did not disappear. He asked me if I knew any Vietnamese masseur. I replied to him that I had massage skills. I could try to give him a massage and if I didn't do it successfully, I would go to find a professional Vietnamese masseur and he agreed. I told him that I needed a bottle of Chinese medicated oil or a can of Tiger Balm. I let him lie face down and I kneaded/rubbed, with my right hand and changed hand when I felt tired, continuously, on his right shoulder blade, where he suffered, with the strong Chinese medicated oil for about half an hour. I didn't utilise any other techniques at all. After I had given him the massage he said he felt a little bit better. The next day, I went to ask him and he replied that he felt 50 percent better.

And a few days later when I saw him again, he told me that he was one hundred percent healed. After that, he took a liking to me and wanted to help me relocate to a Western country as soon as possible.

Now let me go back to my story in prison. The Khmer Rouge chief, who was in charge of the old municipal cadastral survey prison, often gave me rice and dried fish to eat secretly. I then recovered 100 percent from my illness, and I was able to return to work as usual. I did not tell my friend, Thy, about the supplemented food that I was given, because this was a matter of life and death. At that time, I had to use my own tricks or strategies if I wanted to survive. My friend was wondering why my health was back to normal so fast and he rarely saw me eating porridge with the other prisoners! As for my friend, his teeth were black, his body was thin, especially his chest, which was bony, and his belly was swollen and big. It was a sign of starvation. I often saw him when he came back from work in the evening. He hid a young banana tree and he sliced it thinly and mixed it with the watery rice porridge that he was given to eat so that it could fill up his stomach to the full. Since the young banana tree had resin and it would stick to our teeth if we did not clean it with a toothbrush and toothpaste. The programme of the Great Leap Forward of the Khmer Rouge that they copied in its entirety from the failed Chinese communist "Great Leap Forward" utilised in the 1960s did not require people to use toothbrushes and toothpaste. Hence, the Khmer Rouge did not distribute toothbrushes and toothpaste to the new people at all! Did you know that in the era the Khmer Rouge of Democratic Kampuchea, 3 years, 8 months and 20 days, they never distributed toothpaste and toothbrushes to the people, even their own native people? Only some high-ranking cadre members received them. Some people took charcoal, grinding it into powder and using it instead of toothpaste, while others used fingers instead of toothbrushes. I'd like to inform the current generation about this! As for me, in those days I never brushed my teeth. I just brushed my teeth with my fingers with the water from the rice field, river, lake, creek, stream, or whatever the water source I could find.

As for the drinking water, during the months of the dry season and while we were working in the rice fields, the water was scarce and we had to drink it from the water buffalo pools which was as white as condensed milk. I had to drink it because I had no choice – otherwise, my body would be dehydrated and I would have died of thirst!

The Khmer Rouge believed that Western medicines, toothpaste and toothbrushes were not important for nation building because they were useless, but for their high-ranking cadre, they surely used them. I believed that they were all hypocrites, fake people.

I was imprisoned in the old municipal cadastral survey building until the end of October 1975. The

Khmer Rouge planned to close down the prison because it was full and there was no place to put any more prisoners. They would move us to a new place soon. While I was in that prison, I met an old 17 April Chinese man, a fellow prisoner, who did not speak Khmer very fluently because he had come from the Communist China decades ago, and during the Lon Nol era, he said, he was an owner of a large soy sauce factory in Phnom Penh. When the Khmer Rouge evacuated Phnom Penh, he was separated with his wife and children, and he came alone to Battambang province. He travelled without documents, was arrested and imprisoned with me. His name was Seng, I called him "Kong Seng" (Grandfather Seng). He was about 60 years old, and I will tell you later in the book the tragic story of his death in 1976.

18: Kandal Temple

All the prisoners were transferred by the Khmer Rouge to a new location, Kandal Temple, in the east of the old stone bridge. The prisoners travelled on foot without being tied up or handcuffed. They marched north in a long row on Street 1, crossed the old stone bridge, turned left along the banks of the Sangke River, and walked until they reached the temple. The Khmer Rouge soldiers were armed with AK 47 Assault Rifles while escorting all the prisoners to a new location.

When we arrived at the Kandal Temple, the prisoners were not chained, handcuffed, or shackled. Some were put in the old monk dormitory, some were in the old dining hall, and some were in the old seminary, while my friend and I were put in the monk dormitory. The Khmer Rouge just locked the gates of the temple and put guards outside the perimeter of the temple. In the Kandal Temple Prison, there were hundreds of prisoners. My friend and I were allocated to stay in the old dormitory on the left if we entered through the main gate along the bank of the Sangke River. I took a photograph of the dormitory where I stayed more than 20 years ago when I first went back to Cambodia after I left in 1979.

Inside the Kandal Temple, there were many coconut trees. My friend, Thy, and I felt like eating coconuts because for many months I had not eaten them since the Khmer Rouge soldier tortured me at the foot of the coconut tree at the Baktra Orphanage. When I saw a coconut tree with a lot of coconuts, my feet often itched and wanted to climb it, because I already had the skills to climb any type of coconut tree regardless of the height. I did not need to put a string around my feet to help me grip the tree trunk and push upward like other climbers.

One morning, at about 9 o'clock, I picked a coconut tree which I wanted to climb on the east side of the temple, near the fence of the temple, which was about 7 to 8 metres high. It was quiet and far from the eyes of the people. I did not want the other prisoners to see, for fear that they would report it to the Khmer Rouge for their personal gain. I was afraid that I would be caught and tortured again or I would be killed. I trusted only one friend and I no longer trusted others after my bad experience in Phnom Baktra. My friend was watching for me and would alert me if anyone coming our way. I then started to climb the coconut tree. When I reached the top of the coconut tree, I sat on the sixth branch, picked four or five coconuts and dropped them down. Believe it or not, I weighed less than 40 kilograms at that time. I was small and thin, but somehow the branch of the coconut tree was breaking. I quickly reached out and grabbed another branch, but unfortunately, I started to hear the breaking sound again. And I fell from the top of the coconut tree, my buttocks hitting the ground first.

At that time, I felt a very sharp pain in my chest and I began to writhe under the coconut tree. I could not speak and was nearly out of breath. I was in pain all over my body under the palm tree. I asked my friend to rub my chest in order to relieve the pain and lay on the ground under the palm tree for a while. Then I checked my limbs: there was no damage or broken, just chest pain. I thought I was very lucky to be alive. Luckily, because in that regime, if we broke or lost any limb, we would have a hard time, but I was grateful to the Divine Being for helping me to fall my buttocks first. If had fallen head first and hit the ground, I would have broken my neck and died. And if my arms and legs had hit the ground first, I would surely have broken those limbs, because the coconut tree was 7 to 8 metres high. Do you believe that when I was falling, I felt that I had already fainted! I told my friend to take the coconuts that I picked and hide them in a stupa to eat them later, because I could not eat them then. I let my friend help me walk back to my dormitory.

After falling from the top of the coconut tree, I started to have a severe chest pain and my body was aching all over. I could not eat for three days. I did not go to work, and lied to the Khmer Rouge that I had a fever. The Khmer Rouge believed me because I didn't eat porridge for the last three days.

If you believe in Khmer folklore, when you pick fruits in the temple grounds, you should ask the gods who look after the temple first before you pick them, otherwise the gods will punish you lightly, such as falling from the top of a coconut tree, etc. And if it is a serious mistake, such as throwing or damaging an idol/statue in the temple, it may cause you death. About a week later, I went out to pick some milk fruits alone. This time it was in the east of the pagoda. Under the tall milk fruit tree, there was concrete all over, not earth like there was under the coconut tree. If I fell this time, I would certainly die or break my limbs, but this time I asked permission from the gods of the temple first that I was hungry and my body needed to eat, and I did not fall. Do you have the same faith as me?

19: Chork Village

In December 1975, the rice harvest season arrived.
The Khmer Rouge's top-ranking cadre decided to
close the Kandal Temple Prison, perhaps because
they thought that it was useless to keep the prisoners
there if they were not doing any real work. There were
between two to three hundred prisoners and we were
all sent to harvest rice in the village of Chork. Chork
village was located in the southeast of the Battambang
Provincial Town. It was about 36 km from the Kandal
Temple Prison, and in the northeast of Mong Russey
regional town.

On the morning of 1 December 1975, at the front
of the Kandal Temple, there were several trucks lined
up to transport prisoners to Chok village to harvest
rice. As before, the Khmer Rouge did not handcuff,
shackle or chain prisoners. They just let them get on
the trucks and sit quietly. We didn't dare to ask them
any questions. When we arrived at Chok village, the
Khmer Rouge had already built sheds for the prisoners to stay. The sheds were roofed with corrugated
iron sheets. There were about 30 Khmer Rouge soldiers guarding the prisoners. Out of those prisoners,
there were only a few young ones and I was 12 years
old at the time. The commander of the Khmer Rouge
soldiers was called Ta Sok (Grandpa Sok). The prisoners were given enough rice to eat because it was

during the harvest season, but there was no meat or fish to eat at all. When we first arrived at the Chok village in December 1975, they did not impose much discipline. We just went out to harvest rice from 6 am to 11 am, came back to our accommodations, finished lunch at 12 noon, went back to work again and finished off work until 5 pm. We spent exactly 10 hours per day working in the fields, not including meetings and travels from the sheds to the fields.

Prisoners who were older than me were experienced in trapping rice-field rats. They set their traps in the early evening and went back to collect their catches in the early morning before they went to work. Rice-field rats became very large indeed and their bodies were full of fat during the rice harvest season. Some of them weighed almost one kilogram each. I stood and watched older prisoners preparing the rats for cooking. They just skinned them and then marinated them with salt only and grilled them, if they could find salt, because salt was a rare commodity and only the kitchen staff had access to it. Some fried the rats with edible vegetables picked from the rice-fields and used the rat's fat as oil. I just stood there and watched them cooking. Its smell wafted through the air and made my stomach rumble. I was salivating, because I had not eaten red meat for a very long time. The ones who caught rats only ate with each other and they never shared their food with others. During the Pol Pot regime, everyone was on his/her own. The Khmer

Rouge did not have strict rules about finding extra food to eat, but we had to work hard during working hours. We could only look for food outside working hours.

I found myself deficient in vitamins and proteins and needed fresh red meat, vegetables and fruits. As for beef, chicken, and duck, it was clear that there was no way I could find them, but there were a lot of rats all over the fields if I knew how to trap or dig their holes. I was a city dweller with no experience of catching rats at all, but I could learn from the elders because the rat traps were very easy to make and I did not need to go to a vocational school to learn how to make them. The next morning, before going to work, I was walking around the rice fields to see if I could catch a rat with my bare hands, but the rats were so clever that they would not let me catch or hit them easily while I was looking for them. All of a sudden I came across a dead rat lying in the field, I picked and sniffed it, and it smelled a little bit off. I did not know when it had died, so I took it back to my shed, gutted, skinned it and marinated it with salt that I had been secretly hiding since I was in the Kandal Temple Prison. At lunch time, I grilled my marinated rat, and it smelled so good that it made other prisoners swallow their saliva either because they did not want or know how to find them. I ate only one half of my grilled rat and set aside the other half for dinner. This rat meat was amazingly delicious. I did not share it with anyone else and felt proud of finding it myself. Later, I learned how to make rat traps all by myself, by peeking at the elder prisoners' traps. They were very simple. I just cut up plywood about 20cm by 20cm, put heavy dirt on top of the plywood, tied a string with a small stick, used it as a trigger rod and put some rice as bait. All I had to do was to look for the rats' paths, set the trap on a path and when the rats were walking or running or stopping by to eat the baits, the trigger rod would release and the heavy plywood with soil on top would squash the rat and kill it instantly. In the early morning, before going to work, I went to check the rat traps I set the night before. When I opened one of my traps, I suddenly saw a large dead rat, flat like a fried-battered banana and I felt very proud of my achievement. I hid the traps to set them again in the evening because I was afraid they would be stolen.

When I got to my shed, I skinned my priceless rats, removed all the internal organs except the hearts, livers and fat and marinated them with my stash of salt. During lunch time, I either grilled, or stir-fried it, using its fat as oil, with free growing vegetables in the rice fields such as water convolvulus. When I caught more rats than I could eat, I just marinated them with salt and dried them in the sun.

When I started eating rat meat every day, I became healthy and strong, and I worked tirelessly for the Khmer Rouge Organisation, though I had never seen what it/he/she/they looked like. The Khmer Rouge soldiers ate differently from us, the prisoners. Their chefs cooked delicious soup with fish and meat on a regular basis. The Khmer Rouge soldiers never finished their food and there was leftover food every night. I was very close to Ta Sok, the Khmer Rouge chief stationed there. I asked him for salt and he gave me salt. I asked him for the leftover food he gave it to me also, but he only gave it to me and no one else. I called him father. He was very kind and friendly with me, probably because he didn't have any children and took pity on me being an orphan. As for my friend, Thy, he did not know how to talk or to please people. He ate whatever the food Khmer Rouge provided, and he didn't know how to find extra food. When he was living with his family back home in Phnom Penh, before the Khmer Rouge took over the government, he was the son of a rich man who studied in a French private school, had a villa, car with a chauffeur and servants. He didn't live in a wooden house with corrugated iron roofs like my house. And his father was a colonel in the Lon Nol army. Hence, he had no chance interacting with the children of the poor neighbours, so his social experience was close to zero.

The older prisoners sharing the shed with me were very jealous of me, because they saw me eating extra food given by the Khmer Rouge chief, but I did not care at all about them. I had to find ways to get extra food with whatever strategies I could use to survive and to be healthy.

My skin was white, and when I was exposed to the sun for several days in a row without having a long-sleeve shirt, harvesting rice with sickle in the rice fields, it got burned, and after a few days, it had sores, the skin broke and it bled.

At that time, I did not see the Khmer Rouge soldiers killing any prisoners, or they were taken and disappeared. The harvest season in Chork village came to an end in early February 1976. The Khmer Rouge relocated the prisoners to the Chork River and allocated them to build dams and dig canals. After our arrival to this new place, more and more prisoners started to arrive. They had arrested hundreds of ex-Khmer Rouge soldiers from different regions who they thought had committed immorality or betrayal of their Revolutionary Organisation, and brought them to the village of Chork, as well as former ex-Lon Nol soldiers. Hundreds of ex-Lon Nol soldiers who had been sent to Thailand for military training before the Fall of Phnom Penh, 17 April 1975 were sent back from Thailand. Perhaps this was at the request of the government of Democratic Kampuchea, or they were lured to return to rebuild Cambodia, or the Thai government sent them back on their own; I did not know. I often asked those former Lon Nol soldiers about their reasons for returning to Communist Cambodia where they had to work hard for free, endured hardship, ate less, etc. Why they didn't live in Thailand or resettle in the United States or France? They said that they had to return to Cambodia to rebuild their nation. They were patriotic, I supposed.

The Chork village became the largest concentration camp in the Northwest Zone, numbering in the thousands. During the dry season, prisoners actively worked on dams, digging canals, and worked three times a day: from 6 a.m. to 11 a.m., lunch break, from 12 noon to 5 p.m., dinner break, from 6 p.m. to 11 p.m. This meant that we worked for a total of 15 hours per day. Prisoners had to get up very early every morning for the meeting of the whole group; they lined up, did the headcount, then criticised one another in a subgroup to find faults and improve efficiency, then self-criticised for the subgroup to hear. Then we had to sing revolutionary songs (such as the song "Red Blood Reddened in the Field of Cambodia, Motherland..."). All these useless meetings, criticisings, travelling to and from work, we spent another four to five hours a day, which meant that we only had a total of four to five hours of sleep per night, and it was not enough.

During the construction of dams and digging canals during the night, the Khmer Rouge started several generators to illuminate the construction sites. In my sub-sub-group of three, I and another skinny elder prisoner carried the dirt while Kong Seng (Grandfather Seng) dug the ground with a hoe. He was sick, skinny, old and couldn't walk far, so I let him do the digging. We both carried dirt with an instrument made of bamboo called (Pe Le) by hand, one at the front and one at the back. Do you know the word "Pe Le"? I, myself, never heard of this word before the Fall of Phnom Penh in 17 April 1975. I checked it in the dictionary of Samdech Sang Chuon Nath (Edition de L'institute Bouddhique 1967-1968), there was no word for "Pe Le". I did not know where the Khmer Rouge got this word from. It was an instrument made of split bamboos and vines. They initially cut up bamboo poles about 1 metres long, split them up about 1 centimetre wide, used vines to weave them into a mat about 80 centimetres wide, then used vines to tie the four corners to a bamboo pole about 1.2 metres long on each side. That was it. These were very ingenious dirt-carrying instruments created by the Khmer Rouge for two people to carry. They made them for all sizes; a child like me used a small size.

In the rainy season, we were allowed to eat steamed condensed rice in a tin pan, and during the rice harvest season, we were allowed to eat a full meal to our heart's content for about three weeks, and after that we were rationed condensed porridge again. At one time in December 1976, during the rice harvest season, we were allowed to eat freely. I over-ate, and my stomach was so full that I couldn't walk back from the communal canteen to my shed. This was the very first time that happened to me. I felt very uncomfortable. I tried to urinate, defecate and even make myself vomit to relieve the pressure on my stomach, but I was not successful. So, I sat down and slept on the ground for about half an hour or so, and when I felt a little bit better I started to walk very slowly back to my shed. And from then on, I promised myself not be greedy to over-eat again, even if we were allowed to eat freely.

Many of the prisoners who escaped from this concentration camp were shot dead by Khmer Rouge soldiers. It was very hard to escape from this place. The Khmer Rouge did not care at all. During the evening, I and others often saw prisoners being tied up with ropes and marched to their death. The soldiers just blindfolded their eyes with pieces of black cloth, tied their hands with tiny forest vines, and marched them slowly and silently to be killed in the forest near the river bank near our shed. I did not see any prisoner rebel against the Khmer Rouge soldiers. They were easily marched to be slaughtered to the killing fields as easily as killing a flock of sheep. Some soldiers did not even carry guns. Those who were killed were all experienced in life, like the former Lon Nol soldiers who were sent back from Thailand with excellent military training, while the illiterate Khmer Rouge soldiers were not trained at all. If I had been them, I would have broken the thin vines, which even a five-year-old would have been able to break, snatch the guns from the Khmer Rouge soldiers, shoot them, and jump into the flowing river. There were certainly still some chances of survival, because they were going to be killed anyway. All those former Lon Nol soldiers were afraid of the Khmer Rouge and did not dare to do so. What about you, readers? If you were in such a situation, what would you do?

20: Malaria

In June 1976, I developed a severe strand of malaria, and I began to shiver every morning from 11 a.m. to 12 noon for almost two months. The Khmer Rouge did not give me any medicines to take at all. There were no ambulances which could take me to the hospital and there were not any nurses or doctors on site at all. People just died of their treatable diseases in the hundreds. I just boiled young bitter leaves with its flowers picked from the neem trees (*Azadirachta indica*) and sometimes I crushed and squeezed them for its bitter green juice and drank it instead of using the French quinine, which was not given and reserved only for the high-ranking Khmer Rouge cadre.

One day, after a heavy downpour in the rainy season, I was walking from the low zinc roofing shed where we were staying, toward the bank of the river. As I was walking up and down, I spotted a giant snake-headed fish jumping on the ground. I found a piece of wood and beat the fish repeatedly until it died. I then took off my T-shirt, wrapped up the fish and walked back to my shed quietly, for fear of being seen by others.

This giant fish weighed about 4 to 5 kilograms. I did not tell anyone about catching it because I thought God gave it to me alone and I should eat it alone. I did not go looking for this fish, it came for me. My body was emaciated, and I had just recovered from malaria, which had made me shiver every morning. I cut one piece of fish, the tail part, and grilled it. I then ate it with the portion of rice porridge provided and some young tamarind leaves, pounded with a pinch of salt. It tasted amazing. I did not even tell my close friend, Thy, about catching this fish.

I did not marinate the rest of the fish because I did not have much salt left. I just left it as it was. I then took the rest of the fish, wrapped it in big leaves, then in my cotton scarf, and hid it under the zinc roof above where I slept. Three days later, the fish became swollen and rotten. I then cut small pieces of it at a time for grilling and to eat it with my lunch and dinner. The fish smelled exactly like Cambodian traditional fermented fish. About five days later, the fish that God gave me became so smelly that its stench wafted all over the shed. Maybe someone reported it to the chef and that's why he knew where I was hiding it.

From the shed to the workplace was about 4 km away and the chef and cooks had to carry the lunch on bamboo poles to provide for the workers. The food of the day was sour soup with waterlilies, to eat with thick rice porridge. The waterlilies were freely growing in the rice fields. I was very surprised, because this soup contained small pieces of smelly fish and it was very rare for the Khmer Rouge to provide us fish for lunch and dinner. They usually made soup with freely growing vegetables in the rice fields and put it with a bit of salt and fermented fish and that was that! I was very curious and wondering where the hell the chef got the fish from. So, I put a question gently to him about the fish: "Where did you get the fish from to make the soup, which is so delicious, father?" (The words "father" and "grandfather" were respectful terms when addressing seniors and the Khmer Rouge chiefs at that time.)

The chef replied immediately: "It's your fish, Comrade Sao, son!"

I could not believe his words. I became so angry after he said that it was my fish and I wanted to smash his head with the bamboo pole that he used to carry the food with. That fish, I believed strongly, was the fish that God had given me, because God saw that I had nearly died from malaria. If I had smashed him on the head, the Khmer Rouge soldiers would have taken me to be executed immediately. Therefore, I kept my mouth shut and said nothing to him.

The chef also added: "You must not eat privately, son! You must share your fish communally. You are so lucky that I did not report this find to the Khmer Rouge. Otherwise, you would have been severely punished for not sharing your big fish."

I lived in this camp for more than a year. The things that I stole were buried in the ground wrapped up with a plastic bag so that the rain water could not seep through. I did not tell anyone, even my best friend, Thy, about it, because it was a matter of life and death. My buried treasures were mostly salt, fermented fish and tobacco. I started smoking tobacco right after my parents were taken away to be killed. One day I saw the Khmer Rouge soldiers drying tobacco on three sheets of galvanized iron. At night, they did not put it back in their house. They just left it over night to absorb the dew to make it soft, sticky and aromatic. No prisoner dared to steal it from them! If it was stolen, and found it in the possession of prisoners, they would be shot dead immediately, because there was no other prison to send them to, since they were already in prison. At about two o'clock in the morning, I crept out quietly from my shed, and went to collect all the tobacco, leaving not a single strand for the Khmer Rouge to smoke. I buried it in my secret treasure and went back to sleep as if nothing happened. Early in the morning, before leaving for work, the Khmer Rouge searched all the prisoners' belongings for the tobacco that had been stolen during the night. They were very angry indeed. They fought against the Lon Nol and American soldiers and they won the war. Marshal Lon Nol also fled the country before Phnom Penh fell. But they couldn't find the thief that stole their tobacco. If found, that prisoner/thief had to be destroyed by any means! Can you, readers, suggest to the Khmer Rouge how to torture him when caught stealing their tobacco?

We ate lunch and dinner in groups, which consisted of steamed rice or porridge, one bowl for each person, and a large container of soup/stew consisting mostly of vegetables picked from the rice fields, for 11 prisoners. Most of the prisoners did not eat their rationed rice or porridge. They ate only the soup until they finished it and kept their porridge or rice. Then they ate with whatever they could find in the rice fields, such as crabs, snails, fish, snakes, crickets or rats. I always had my reserve food or sauce. If I could find small rice field crabs, I pounded them raw and alive with young tamarind or tamarind sprouts and put a bit of my prized fermented fish and a bit of salt obtained from my treasure. I used it little by little and no one knew, because I already learnt my lesson for stealing coconuts at the foot of the Baktra Mountain. I ate it with my rice, raw or wrapped it with leaves and grilled it. My tobacco was the same. I smoked it little by little, and it lasted me for almost a year.

21: Two prisoners

In Chork village the Khmer Rouge organised prisoners into groups, subgroups and subsubgroups. The chief and deputy chief of the group looked after three subgroups which consisted of eleven each. The chief and the deputy chief of the subgroup looked after three subsubgroups which consisted of three each. The chief of the subsubgroup looked after two persons, a total of 35 men and women in each group. I was very active, hardworking and never complained to the Khmer Rouge soldiers about the working conditions, so they assigned me to be a chief of a subsubgroup, in charge of two persons. At that time I was 13 years old.

One of these prisoners was called Kong Seng, 60 years old, and the other was called Ram Rai, 30 years old. But Ram Rai's face was very old and wrinkled like Kong Seng, because he was chronically ill and was very thin. His ribs were exposed and bony, and there was not much flesh at all. If either of them escaped, I had to report immediately to the chief of my subgroup, then the chief of my subgroup had to report to the chief of the group, then the chief of the group had to report to Khmer Rouge soldiers occupying there. And then the soldiers were despatched to pursue them, and when they had caught them, they would shoot and kill them.

There was one time, during the anniversary of the Khmer Rouge's victory, when prisoners were allowed to travel to Kakoh village to celebrate and eat a full meal. It was delicious, with chunks of beef, and we even had dessert. My skinny body really needed those proteins and sugar. But when we were about to line up and go back to our shed, one of the two prisoners that I had to supervise, Ram Rai, suddenly disappeared. I reported him missing to my subgroup leader. My subgroup leader was kind enough not to report him missing to the group leader and he immediately sent me to search for him. After a while, I found him stealing fermented fish and palm sugar hidden in his shirt. I told him to drop all those things for fear that the Khmer Rouge would see him in possession of those things and kill him. He then followed my advice. When we arrived back at the meeting point, my subgroup leader just kicked him a few times, gave him a warning and did not report it to the Khmer Rouge. Ram Rai was very lucky not to be killed at that time.

Hundreds of Khmer Rouge soldiers ran that concentration camp of Chak-Ka Koh. Prisoners could not escape. I saw men or Lon Nol veterans who had been trained in Thailand in military tactics and combats. They were very skilful, but when they escaped, they were caught all the time and the Khmer Rouge soldiers just shot and killed them all.

In 1976, I was 13 years old and I had my own escape strategy and plan that I had observed over the year. I wanted to make it a successful escape because I saw the Khmer Rouge had a gap in their prevention of prisoners' escapes. If I escaped, I would not let the Khmer Rouge catch and kill me. I did not tell anyone about my easiest way to escape, even my close friend. I still wished to escape to Battambang Provincial Town and continue my journey to Thailand, even though I had been living here for almost a year then.

Now I would like to talk about the story of Kong Seng, the prisoner who I had to supervise. The Khmer Rouge believed that he had a lot of things in his possession because in his bag he had everything. He had monosodium glutamate and a sewing needle and thread that he had brought with him since he left Phnom Penh. He used his monosodium glutamate very sparingly, only a few pellets at a time. He had a lot of blankets and old clothes. At around three o'clock in the morning, he would often moan loudly, pretending to have a fever, because he knew the Khmer Rouge would blow their whistle to wake the prisoners up at 4 o'clock, get them to line up, and sing revolutionary songs, such as the song "Red Blood..." and count the number of prisoners to check if any of them were missing or not. We had to listen to their repetitive speeches and how great their Revolutionary Organisation was, and they asked us to criticise one another and self-criticise during the meeting.

At 5 am, we started to go to work in the fields because the workplace was far from the dormitory and we started working from 6 am onwards until lunch time. The Khmer Rouge allowed those who knew how to smoke tobacco to rest, and if any prisoners did not know how to smoke, they had to work until the whistle blew. So I had to learn how to smoke fast in order to have smoke breaks. Kong Seng, when he shivered every now and then, would only shake his legs; from his waist to his head he would not shake at all. He used his old blanket that I had never seen him wash it at all to cover both of his legs, and if it was during daytime when he was shivering, he sewed his clothes with the sewing needle he had brought from Phnom Penh. The Khmer Rouge did not believe that he was genuinely sick. They said that he was faking his illness; since they had fought for many years with the Lon Nol soldiers, they had never seen anyone with malaria trembling only in his/her legs while the upper body and arms did not tremble at all. The Khmer Rouge had their own slogans or poems at that time, translated literally as: fever, chills, tractor fever, car fever, food fever and moral fever. I still remember this Khmer Rouge poem till this day, after 46 years.

One day, Kong Seng, told me that he was too sick to go to work. When I went to work and saw wild spider flowers (*Cleome Gynandra L*), I should not forget to pick some for him because he wanted to make pickled wild spider flowers so that we could share it together.

One day, the Khmer Rouge assigned the prisoners to build earthen dams, and we had to dig and carry the soil quite a distance to the dam. The Khmer Rouge soldiers walked up and down to watch the prisoners working. If anyone worked slowly, he/she would be reprimanded. At that time, they saw Kong Seng slowly digging the soil and putting it in a Pe Le, which I and Ram Rai had to carry to the dam about 3 metres high. Kong Seng was then reprimanded by them for working too slowly. The Khmer Rouge said, "Kong Seng, you work too slowly! I'll hit you with a truncheon (literally 'bull's penis' in Khmer) if you don't speed it up!" Kong Seng was very angry with the Khmer Rouge at the time. He was more than 60 years old, in poor health, malnourished, emaciated and separated from his wife and children since the Fall of Phnom Penh on 17 April 1975. He didn't know whether they were dead or alive. He also told me that when our country was free from the Khmer Rouge Regime, he would adopt me, let me go to school to complete my education and have a good future. He was no longer afraid of the Khmer Rouge, maybe he did not want to live anymore. He replied to the Khmer Rouge soldiers with a Chinese accent, "You motherfucker, I'm not even afraid of the penis of a horse and you think that I'm afraid of the truncheon (bull's penis)!" The Khmer Rouge did not respond to him at all. They just pretended to be indifferent because they used psychology, then they left. But the other prisoners and I were next to him and heard him say those swear words to the Khmer Rouge, thinking that maybe he would be taken away and killed that night, because no prisoner would ever dare to swear at the Khmer Rouge. Later that evening, after dinner, I and other prisoners saw two Khmer Rouge soldiers with guns in their hands, calling Kong Seng to pack his belongings and escort him to study. During the Khmer Rouge's era, the word 'study' meant to kill. The day after Kong Seng was summoned by the Khmer Rouge to study, the prisoners sleeping in the shed could no longer hear him moaning with his faked malaria. I would like to pray for the soul of Mr. Kong Seng to rest in peace, so that he would no longer endure hardships in the Khmer Rouge Regime. They made him work like an animal, they did not provide him enough food to eat, they separated him from his wife and his children, and they didn't even bury him with a proper grave so that his descendants (if they are still alive) could go and pray for him at his grave.

I told my friend, Thy, about my escaped plan. If he didn't want to go with me, I would not care because I had had enough of this place. I would escape alone, because I had a lot of stress of daily heavy work. We worked like cattle: no freedom, not enough nutritious food to eat, and no real vegetables. Every day we ate only vegetables which grew freely in the rice fields and turned our teeth black like charcoal, and especially there was no future at all for me. My friend thought about my plan for a few days and agreed to escape with me. I never pressured him to come along with me, but my plan was to keep it a secret so that no one would know. If the Khmer Rouge knew about our plan first, they would catch us and when they caught us and they would shoot us dead for sure. I thought that the Khmer Rouge were very intelligent and cunning because they had won the war and defeated Lon Nol's army as well. We, the prisoners, also had brains because we were human beings as well. Normally, when a person in the group was missing, the group leader had to report to the Khmer Rouge soldiers immediately, otherwise the leaders of the group, subgroup and subsubgroup would be shot because the Khmer Rouge would think that we had conspired with the escapees. Human lives, at that time, were considered by the Khmer Rouge like rats because they thought that we were useless and cattle were more valuable than humans because they could plough the fields. One early evening, as we were about to return to our lodgings, we did not stand in a line to be counted. The rice fields in the Chork-Kakoh village were vast and the rice plants were more than a metre high because the soil there was very fertile. It would be difficult for the Khmer Rouge to search for the escapees since the area was so large. It would take hundreds of people to search, or they might think that we both ran to National Road 5 or ran to the railway tracks because there were two roads leading to the Provincial Town of Battambang. I had been observing the Khmer Rouge's tactic of catching the escapees: as soon as a prisoner disappeared, the Khmer Rouge despatched their special forces to chase and ambush them along both roads. I had lived there for more than a year, and had never seen the Khmer Rouge capture and bring escapees back. The penalty for any escapee was to be shot there on the spot. Rarely, those older escapees successfully escaped and were caught most of the time. And when they were caught they would be brutally killed, but my 13-year-old brain had a different approach from anyone else. When it came to using it, it was very easy and I did not need to go to study in France like the former Khmer Rouge leaders such as: Pol Pot, Ieng Sary, Khieu Samphan, Son Sen, Khieu Ponnary, Khieu Thirith, etc.

Let me add another story about my times in that concentration camp. When I first arrived at the village of Chork, I saw with my own eyes the skeletons of Lon Nol's soldiers. There were hundreds of corpses lying unburied in the middle of the rice field. Almost all them were rotten and only the skeletons and the clothes were left. How I could identify them because of their uniforms of Paramilitary and American MikeForce military shoes. I picked up a few shoes and shook them up, and out came the foot bones. The Lon Nol soldiers who were killed there were probably taken by the Khmer Rouge from the Battambang Provincial Town to receive or welcome the Prince Father/ Sihanouk in Phnom Penh.

Now, let me go back to my story. We both crouched down in the rice paddies until dark and then we got up to smoke tobacco. As for the light, I used a small piece of iron and a small stone, which gave sparks when I stroked these two pieces together. When the sparks hit the cotton, it started to emit smoke so that I could light my tobacco rolls. If there was sunlight, I would use a reading glass that I had exchanged with another prisoner. When I put the glass against the sunlight for a while, the white light emitted through the glass would be hot and when it hit the cotton it would start to burn so that I could light my tobacco rolls. These were my two ways of lighting my tobacco rolls.

After midnight, we felt hungry and started walking to the communal mess to search for food. When we arrived, the chefs/cooks were all asleep because they were tired from working hard during the day, so it was easy for both of us to check in the kitchen. Edible things such as dried fish and bananas were reserved for the Khmer Rouge cadre, because they were citizens of the first class. We just took enough food to eat for two days, and did not want to take too much so that the chefs/cooks would not notice the items were missing and report it to the Khmer Rouge.

We didn't leave for the Battambang Provincial Town immediately, we just hid ourselves in the same village. We wanted to let the Khmer Rouge take their time to find us, and let them become tired. They must have thought that these two children knew how to divert their attention very well. They never went to war and they lost these two kids and they did not know where to find them. From dawn to dusk, we both slept quietly in the thickets of the forest along the river-bank, walking out only at night. We both went out of hiding to steal food from the communal mess for three consecutive nights.

22: Anlong Vil Village

After midnight on our third night of hiding, Thy and I started to make our way towards National Road 5 and continued our journey to the Provincial Town of Battambang. I guessed after we disappeared from the group, the Khmer Rouge soldiers probably searched for us for at least a day, but I gave them an extra day just in case I was wrong. I also did not dare to stay in our hiding spot for too long and thought that three nights should be enough. I was one hundred percent correct in my estimate. When we both left for the Battambang Provincial Town, we did not encounter any Khmer Rouge soldiers at all. At dawn, we walked along the National Road 5, and when we walked close to villages, we just skirted around them to the fields or the forest for fear that the village chiefs or the Khmer Rouge soldiers would question us. We slept in the forest at night time. Then we ran out of food.

The next day we started our journey again. As we arrived at the village of Chumnik near Anlong Vil village and we saw a tody/sugar palm tree with several canisters made of bamboo for collecting the tody palm juice on top of the tree. I told my friend to wait for me under the sugar palm tree and if anyone came, just shout to alert me, then I would quickly descend from the tree top and would run away and not be caught. I started to climb the sugar palm tree. It felt much easier than climbing the coconut trees, because there was a bamboo pole with its short branches for stepping on and the pole was tied securely around the tree trunk. When I reached the top of the palm tree, I started drinking a tube of sugar palm juice, because I was hungry and thirsty and I did not eat the previous evening. The sugar palm juice was delicious and very sweet and it energised me straight away. I untied three tubes: one for my friend to drink now, and we would take the other two tubes for the road. I tied the three tubes around my waist and began to come down but when I reached the base of the sugar palm tree, I was surprised because there was a Khmer Rouge solodier standing under the tree, and my friend, Thy, was nowhere to be found. I really did not know where he was. He was supposed to keep an eye for me and he did not give me any signs to alert me at all. He was probably scared and ran away to hide as soon as he saw a soldier approaching. The soldier began to question me where I was travelling to and asked to see my travel documents. I told him that I didn't have any. As before, I told him the same story that I was looking for my parents and siblings who had been separated since the Fall of Phnom Penh in April 1975. While I was being questioned, I suddenly saw my friend came out of his hiding spot in a nearby banana plantation so that he would be arrested with me and not separated, because we had been struggling together since 1975. I was very angry with my friend but I didn't utter any words to him. My plan to flee to Thailand was now doomed again! This was the second time that my friend let to the Khmer Rouge arresting me, and I did not know how many more times he would ruin my plans in the future!

The Khmer Rouge soldier did not even give my friend the sugar palm juice to drink that I brought down. We were both tied up and taken to The Kandek Temple, west of Anlong Vil village. Once we got there, they told us to grind rice for almost a day and then we were sent to a Khmer Rouge soldiers' house in Svay Kang village on National Road 5. When we arrived at the house of the Khmer Rouge soldiers, I did not see any prisoners, but I did see the barbed wire at the bottom of the house, and the soldiers just put us on the ground floor. All the Khmer Rouge soldiers there carried AK-47 rifles in their hands, but they went out to work in the rice fields every day. I thought this was a place where temporary prisoners were kept. We both stayed there for about three nights and we were told that we would be transferred elsewhere. We did not know the geography of the Battambang Province at all because we were born in Phnom Penh and didn't study any geography in class. The second day we did not have lunch. Maybe the Khmer Rouge soldiers forgot to give us food to eat before they went to work or they wanted to starve us, because at lunch time I did not see them return home to eat until the evening, when I saw them returning from the fields. As soon as they arrived back from the rice fields, my friend complained to the Khmer Rouge soldiers that he did not eat lunch. After he did this, a soldier jumped up and kicked my friend severely several times and he said to my friend, "I just came back from rice fields and I am very tired, and now you want me to cook for you straight away!" I did not dare to complain to the Khmer Rouge. If I did that, they would hate us even more. People, usually, would not die going without food for a day or two.

On the second day we were there, I saw a young female Khmer Rouge soldier come and cook for the soldiers. We were shackled to the pole of the house the whole time we were there. She asked if any of us knew how to climb a tamarind tree, and I raised my hand. She made me promise her that if she unshackled me, I should not run away and I agreed. I climbed a big tamarind tree near the house and picked tamarind buds and fruits for the beautiful young Khmer Rouge soldier. If I wanted to run away, I could do it because I did not see her carry a gun, but if I ran away I would have to leave my friend behind, who was sitting on the ground with a sour face. When he was living with his parents in Phnom Penh, his family had a servant to cook for his family and wash his clothes. He ate Western-style sandwiches with pure butter and beef/pork/chicken patties. The family had a big refrigerator full of food and all kinds of drinks. He could eat any time he wanted. He listened to foreign songs because he had French ancestry and came from a rich family, but now he could only find fermented fish and salt to eat with his meals. He must have thought that his situation had been changed 180 degrees. The young female Khmer Rouge soldier was not stupid either. She released me, and left my friend tied up as if she had bought an insurance policy. So if one ran away, the other one who was being shackled would be punished severely. Therefore, I should not run away! When I got down from the tamarind tree, I took the sprouts/buds and tamarind fruits to her and she shackled me back onto the pole.

I would like to tell you another story. This story is true, because there were hundreds of witnesses and it has been told in other books as well. It occurred in the port of Neak Leung town in April 1975. After the Khmer Rouge evacuated residents from Phnom Penh, the head of an aristocratic (or just rich) family drove his car to the port of Neak Leung, which was loaded with his parents, his wife, and his children. He drove his car straight into the fast-flowing Mekong River, committing suicide with his whole family. He may have thought that he had a chance to get out and leave the country before 17 April yet he stayed behind and believed in the radio propaganda broadcast from Beijing, like my own father. He was thinking that our country would be peaceful and be free from war, and we would free to travel to the provinces and towns after the government of Marshall Lon Nol collapsed, and there would be no more bombings and deaths. My own father and millions of others were cheated. Millions of people died and hundreds of thousands of children became orphans like me.

23:   Samrong Temple Prison

On the fourth day, as Thy and I were still being detained in the Svay Kang village, near Chumnik village and Anlong Vil village, southeast of Battambang Provincial Town, about 7 km from New Stone bridge, Battambang City, two Khmer Rouge soldiers brought an old American military Jeep to take us away. Both of us were told that they would take us to the Samrong Temple. We both did not know where the Samrong Temple was located because we were not from Battambang Province and did not know the geography of this province at all. I guessed that the Samrong Temple was probably a cooperative and they would just let us go to work there. The Samrong Knong Temple is a 300-year-old temple built by the family of Aphai Vong, ex-governor of Battambang Province. This temple is about 4 km from the base of the New Stone Bridge, Battambang Provincial Town and it is in the northwest of Battambang Provincial Town.

The Khmer Rouge soldiers did not handcuff the two of us, they just let us ride normally, like being driven in a taxi. We were looking at the scenery of the districts, villages and Battambang regions. The two soldiers asked us where we were from, why we drifted to the Battambang Province. I said to them, "Elder brother comrade, my friend and I both have been travelling to many provinces to search for our parents and siblings. We have been separated since our country was liberated on 17 April 1975, and now we are in Battambang Province, in case we see all of them again, because we miss them very much." Both soldiers appeared to be meek, gentle, friendly, and kind-hearted. They acted as if they liked to help orphans like us.

When the car arrived in front of the Samrong Knong Temple, one of the soldiers guarding it opened the gate and the car came to a stop in front of an old wooden house. The soldiers who came with me went to talk to the Khmer Rouge soldiers who were running the place. The soldiers stationed at the temple let us wait for a while and then let us both get out of the car. I saw a group of more than 10 Khmer Rouge soldiers and two females. Maybe both of them were cooks for those soldiers, I did not know.

In this temple, it was so quiet, and I didn't hear the sound of people talking at all. I was wondering why they put us both in this temple, why didn't they take us to the cooperative to work in the rice paddies! The Khmer Rouge soldiers ordered the two of us to follow them to the old Dining Hall on the north side of the temple, and they unlocked the door of the Dining Hall. As soon as the door was opened, I sensed a foul smell of faeces and urine. Then they ordered us to go inside. I was shocked and terrified because in this building, I saw all the prisoners with their legs shackled. Each of the U-shaped shackles had two holes on the top ends, and when the shackles were put on the ankles and a long bar was inserted through the two holes, the prisoners could not walk and became stationary. The prisoners slept with their heads against the wall, and they slept in long rows on all four sides of the hall. Most of the prisoners were emaciated, with deep eye-sockets, skinny cheekbones and ghostly eyes, and some of them had just arrived and appeared healthy. All the prisoners looked at me with great pity, because in this prison there were no child-prisoners at all. Maybe this was the first time they had seen children in this prison. The Khmer Rouge soldiers started picking up the U-shaped shackles from a large pile for us. They put one shackle on my friend first, then it was my turn, but it was difficult to find a smaller shackle for me because all the shackles they made were to fit for seniors only. I was allowed to sleep at the beginning of the row, near the door. The wall was facing west, and next to that there was a large water jar for placing prisoners' faeces. Where I slept, that jar of faeces was only about a metre away. Would you, readers, be able to stand the smell of faeces if you are forced to sleep and smell the faeces for three nights and three days in a row, and the open jar of faeces cracks and the faeces mixed with urine has soaked into your clothes when you wake up in the morning?

In each row, old ammunition containers made of steel were placed for the prisoners to defecate and urinate. When the containers were full, one of the prisoners collected them and poured into the jar next to where I slept. When the jar of poo was full, the prisoners were to empty it and carried it to make fertilisers in the banana plantation behind the temple. The Khmer Rouge Revolutionary Organisation did not throw anything away, not even the faeces and urine! For lunch and dinner, liquid rice porridge was distributed to the prisoners, about two scoops of coconut ladle, eaten with salt. No breakfast was given in the morning, so the prisoners' bodies were bony like skeletons. There were two prisoners that the Khmer Rouge assigned to cook the rice porridge for all the prisoners in this temple prison. The next morning, on the second day, the Khmer Rouge soldiers unshackled both of us and assigned us to sweep the rubbish inside the temple grounds. After sweeping, they put the shackles back on us.

Every night I saw the disappearance of old prisoners, who were replaced by new ones. At that time I still did not know why. For three nights I was shackled and both of us were allowed to sweep the temple grounds every morning. In the fourth morning after we arrived at the Samrong Temple Prison, we both were assigned to work as porridge cooks. I wondered where the two prisoners who used to cook porridge were, and I did not dare to ask the Khmer Rouge this question. I had learned from other people that when the Khmer Rouge Organisation assigned us to do something, we did not need to ask them for the reason, because the

Organisation was in charge of taking care of us, even though most of the Khmer Rouge did not know who their Organisation was.

My daily job with my friend was to cook liquid rice porridge for all the prisoners at the Samrong Temple Prison. They set the amount of rice for us to cook every time for the prisoners, and I did not dare to put extra or less rice for fear of severe punishment. There was a small building near the Dining Hall where I cooked the porridge and when the porridge was cooked, I had to put it in two big water containers and then carried them with a bamboo pole with strings attached to distribute to the prisoners every day. The Khmer Rouge soldiers stopped shackling both of us, and they let us both sleep on a wooden bed under a wooden house, while the Khmer Rouge soldiers slept and worked on the first floor. I did not dare to go up the house because it was forbidden, until they requested me to get something. I tried to adapt my attitude to make all those Khmer Rouge soldiers like me and I did not dare to argue with them at all so that I could survive, eat and live comfortably. I also did not dare to ask them when I heard the loud screams coming from a building east of the Dining Hall, because I saw almost every morning the prisoners who were escorted to that place, then I heard the prisoners shouting/screaming/moaning. I thought that maybe the prisoners were being tortured. I often saw prisoners being escorted to the banana plantation in the north corner outside the fence of the temple and after a while, I saw the Khmer Rouge return but did not see the prisoners they took returning with them. So, I concluded that maybe all the prisoners they took were killed.

In the morning, I often saw the Khmer Rouge soldiers drying human gallbladders in the sun, tying them with strings to dry them like drying fish. The human gallbladders of the great Organisation of Democratic Kampuchea, and of the Great Leap Forward, were very valuable. When people used them in a drink, this replaced quinine, and their malaria would disappear. I used to have malaria but never tried it. I just heard people say it, whether it was effective or not, I did not know.

I did not see the female Khmer Rouge soldiers who used to be cooks for the Khmer Rouge soldiers, the male Khmer Rouge soldiers just cooked for themselves. Probably the two of them returned to their village without me knowing it. As for the liquid rice porridge I cooked for the prisoners in the Samrong Temple Prison, I no longer wanted to eat it. When the Khmer Rouge soldiers finished eating their meals, they always let both of us eat the leftovers. Prisoners like us did not have the right to eat with the Khmer Rouge soldiers. We both did not care if we were treated like dogs to eat the leftovers because they were delicious, nutritious and filling! The Khmer Rouge soldiers' cuisine was always delicious, containing fresh grilled fish, soup, dried fish, and often with beef, chicken, duck, or pork. They only ate pure, solid rice, not liquid rice porridge with salt like us prisoners. We both ate the leftovers from the Khmer Rouge soldiers, and our stomachs were full every day, just like living with our parents before the Khmer Rouge took over the government.

My plan to flee to Thailand for my future and freedom was put on hold for the moment because each attempted escape had been unsuccessful. Every time I tried to escape, I was caught, put in prison, became miserable and hungry. I did not know the way exactly and, importantly, I had been caught because of my friend's stupidity. I never gave up my hope to escape to Thailand. I still always hoped that one day I would try again, but then my work here was light, I ate good and delicious leftover food, slept well and was healthy.

In the Samrong Temple Prison, there were many fruit trees, such as a banana plantation just outside the fence of the temple in the eastern corner which was full of ripe bananas. No one dared to come to the south of the area. There was a big gandaria/plum mango tree with sweet yellow fruits. The Khmer Rouge just left them to ripen and fall on the ground, rotten. In the south, near the gate of the temple, there was another type of sour plum mango tree full of yellow fruits as big as chicken eggs. Their yellow fruits made us want to pick them and eat them. There were many other coconut trees near the pond of the temple. Every day, I always climbed the plum mango tree to pick and eat them because their fruits were very sweet and delicious. Sometimes I walked to the banana plantation outside the fence of the temple to pick and eat sweet bananas. I did not ask the Khmer Rouge for permission, I just ate the fruits myself and never brought them back to my accommodation so they wouldn't know.

In the banana plantation outside the pagoda, there were large pits, and I saw freshly killed prisoners all over the pits. The Khmer Rouge took all the prisoners and must have killed them with a hoe or a knife or a solid bamboo tube, because I never heard the sounds of gunshots. They removed their gallbladders as well. The Khmer Rouge did not care about burying the corpses. When I looked down and I saw dead bodies lying in the pits, it seemed to me that maybe they thought that the next night they would kill the new prisoners and did not want to waste their energy burying them. They probably planned that, when the pit was full, they would fill it in once and then dig a new one.

Sometimes human livers were cooked together with fish sauce, and the temple was filled with the smell. I was sure that the prisoners smelt it too because the place where they cooked was not far from the Dining Hall. They just didn't know that it was the livers from their fellow prisoners. This was the regime of Democratic Kampuchea, led by the great and wise Revolutionary Organisation. No other nation experienced what Cambodia did, led by the so-called Communist fanatics. A few millions people died as a result of malnutrition, starvation, and homicide. In this regime, I only saw the Khmers themselves killing one another. I did not see any other nationalities killing the Khmer people! It was only later I learned that the Khmer Rouge leaders were just the ignorant young students. Their parents were unable to send their children to study abroad, and they received free government scholarships without spending any money out of their own pockets. France and the government of Cambodia paid for all the students to study in France in the 1940s and '50s. Some students returned to Cambodia empty-handed without obtaining any degrees, especially Pol Pot and Ieng Sary. When the two of them arrived in France, they did not try to study, get a degree, and get a good education to work for the government of Cambodia. Instead, they studied Communist-Marxist-Leninist theory. Pol Pot, alias Saloth Sar, was Ieng Sary's brother-in-law. Two sisters also studied in France: Khieu Ponnary, who was married to Pol Pot, and Khieu Thirith, who married Ieng Sary. They lived comfortably until the day of their death, except for Pol Pot, who died like a dog in the Thai-Cambodian border in 1998. It was karma, I suppose. Pol Pot and Ieng Sary returned to Cambodia empty-handed, with no bachelor's, master's or doctoral degrees. Other students who completed their doctoral degrees were just as stupid. They were just foolish people returning from France. They did not try to help to rebuild the economy for our country to grow, but instead they destroyed it. More than seven million Cambodian people were used for their experiments. They did not look at the surrounding developed countries and see how their countries had prospered. They only blamed other nations. Before they died, none of them accepted the mistakes they had made. These were the Khmer Rouge, these were the ones who ordered more than two million people in Phnom Penh to evacuate to work in the rice fields with their bare hands without any modern equipment. They did not need to have bachelor's degrees or to have studied in France at all. If people had to evacuate, they should have evacuated gradually and been provided with enough food, medicines, and shelters so that people did not die uselessly. Let me conclude these remarks about the Khmer Rouge Organisation, led by stupid students from France. Now I would like to continue narrating my imprisonment at the Samrong Temple Prison.

My daily work in the Samrong Temple Prison was the easiest. After cooking liquid rice porridge and cleaning/sweeping the temple grounds, I had a lot of free time. Sometimes the Khmer Rouge soldiers, after beating and torturing the prisoners, came back and were exhausted, probably suffering from sore hands and legs. They also asked me to massage them. Sometimes they asked me to pluck their armpit hair, sometimes they asked me to wash their underwear during my time there. When the Khmer Rouge soldiers told me to do whatever, I obeyed. I never hesitated or argued with them, because my precious life depended entirely on them. If they wanted to kill me, they could have done it any time they wanted and I wouldn't have been able to write this story.

In about March 1977, during the early evening, the Khmer Rouge soldiers arrested a man and brought him to the Samrong Temple Prison. The prisoner was wearing a white T-shirt, black trousers and a watch. His hands were tied behind his back. For the first time, in three months, since I came to this prison, I had never seen prisoners being tortured under the wooden house where the Khmer Rouge soldiers were living, next to the wooden bed where I slept. They usually tortured the prisoners in a building next to where I cooked the porridge for prisoners. They took prisoners for questioning in that building, so I did not know why they brought this new prisoner to be interrogated under the wooden house. The Khmer Rouge soldiers surrounded the prisoners, beating him in a circle, interrogating him, kicking him, using their knees, fists and elbows, and slapped him ruthlessly. The prisoner was questioned about his background, his name, what he used to do in the old society, etc. I slept on the wooden bed with my friend about two to three metres away from the place where the newly brought prisoner was being tortured. I could hear and see everything. We both pretended to be asleep, trembling all over our bodies, because our lives were completely dependent on the Khmer Rouge, and if they wanted to kill us, they surely could. All they had to do was just accuse us of betraying their Revolutionary Organisation, and our fate was sealed! These Khmer Rouge were the representatives of the Khmer Rouge Revolutionary Organisation which introduced the policy of the Great Leap Forward (this term was entirely copied by Pol Pot from Chinese Communist President Mao Zedong). The prisoner told his interrogators that his name was Chhuon Chhay, a movie actor and director from the old society. His house was in Prek Khpop village, which was about a few kilometres north of the Samrong Temple Prison at the river bank of the Sangker River. When he was being interrogated, the Khmer Rouge only asked questions if he worked for the CIA or the KGB. The Khmer Rouge tortured Mr Chhuon Chhay by wrapping his head in a plastic bag so that he couldn't breathe. He was choking, then had a fit and fell on the ground because his hands were still being tied behind his back. He lost consciousness. While he was unconscious, his torturers untied the plastic bag, to allow him to breathe normally, and poured water on him to bring him back to consciousness. They beat and tortured Mr Chhuon Chai for almost three hours, and then they escorted him to be slaughtered. After a while, the Khmer Rouge soldiers brought back his liver, chopped it up into bite-sized pieces, fried it and poured over fish sauce. The smell wafted all over the temple. The prisoners at the Dining Hall must have smelled human liver being cooked as well but they probably didn't know exactly what was being cooked. Their distance was only ten metres away from the wooden house. Readers, please consider: was the killing of human beings and the removal of their livers and gallbladders an order from another nation?

My friend and I continued to cook porridge for the prisoners at the Samrong Temple Prison until June 1977, which meant that my friend and I spent almost six months in this prison. The Khmer Rouge cadre decided to close the Samrong Temple Prison. We were both worried about our lives and did not know what the Khmer Rouge had decided about us. Would they kill us? Would they transfer us to another prison, or would they let us work in any cooperative? Before the Khmer Rouge closed the Samrong Temple Prison, the Khmer Rouge soldiers increased the killing rate of prisoners every night, and they killed almost all of them. The remaining ten prisoners or so were trans-ferred to another prison called "Kach Roteh Prison". The Kach Roteh Prison was a local prison, while the Samrong Temple Prison was a prison of the Northwest Region. This new prison was about 28 km southeast of the Samrong Temple Prison on the National Road 5. After the Samrong Temple Prison was closed, I saw a Khmer Rouge cadre member drive a Jeep and stop inside the temple. He told both of us to pack up and go to our new place. I believe that the Khmer Rouge did not want to kill me because I was 14 years old at the time and worked as a cook for the prisoners, strictly obeying the rules of the Organisation. Perhaps the Revolutionary Organisation thought they could brainwash me.

Let me tell you a little story about carrying porridge and spilling half of it. One rainy day, I boiled porridge and put it in two large pots. I started to put a load on my shoulder and carried it only a few steps, but then I fell down because of the slippery ground and almost spilled everything. I could not go and ask for more rice from the Khmer Rouge soldiers to cook again for fear of being accused of reckless work or destroying the Organisation, and also for fear of being tortured. I then decided to put all the remaining porridge back into the pot, added more water and cooked it again. As for the porridge I spilled, I dug up and buried it in the ground, covered with leaves, as if nothing had happened. As I was carrying porridge into the Dining Hall, where the prisoners were being held, one of them shouted at me, "Asao (my revolutionary name)! I saw you spilled the porridge, and I will report it to the Khmer Rouge!" I was sure that he looked at me through a hole in the window while I was cooking the porridge. I was very scared and whispered to him, "Let me give you an extra ladle of the porridge and do not open your mouth." I shouted back to him, "No spilling, I just slipped and fell"! I shouted this lie for other prisoners to hear so that they would not report it to the Khmer Rouge. I was so relieved. I did this because I wanted to live, even though I knew what I did was completely wrong, but who wants to be killed?

24: Omani Village

The Khmer Rouge cadre member who drove the Jeep took me to the Norea village near the banks of the Sangker River, just over a kilometre Southwest of Samrong Temple Prison. The Khmer Rouge cadre member there was called Dek and he was also known as "Ta Dek". He was the head of District 41. The District Office 41 was in front of the Norea Temple, on the corner of Street 153 today. Where I lived and worked was the Commercial Department of District 41. The job was to distribute fish, rice, and salt to the villages and communes in District 41. This was a lucrative job. In the Commercial Department, there was a fish warehouse, rice warehouse and salt warehouse, and no other villagers knew what we were eating. At that time, the Northwest Zone was still led by the Secretary of the Northwest Zone, Ros Nhim. After Pol Pot summoned Ros Nhim to a meeting in Phnom Penh, Pol Pot ordered his execution. Then Ta Mok, Secretary of the Southwest Zone, came to occupy the Northwest Zone.

About a month after I was released from the Samrong Temple prison by the Khmer Rouge, Ta Dek sent six children to a village near Chak-Kokoh, Mong Russey, by horse-drawn carriages. We set out in these carriages to get nearly a hundred cattle to take back to Norea village. We had to spend more than an hour from Norea village to the cowshed because the wagons were fully loaded and heavy, and the horses were small and could not run fast. When they were tired, they just walked very slowly, and we had to get off the carriages. When our group reached our destination, after a short journey, we rested for a while and began to herd the cattle back on National Road Five for almost three hours. When we reached Anlong Vil village, we turned right through Omani village.

Before leaving Norea village, I felt unwell and had a temperature. I did not report this to the Khmer Rouge leaders, because they might accuse me of faking. After herding the cattle for more than an hour, I felt dizzy, my body started to get very hot and I had a severe headache as well. I did not tell children in my group that came with me about it. When the herd reached Omani village, I could not move forward any longer and fell asleep under an orange tree by the roadside. After a while, I also felt a burning sensation all over my body as I was laying on the ground.

As I was sleeping under the orange tree, two Khmer Rouge soldiers came to wake me up and asked me why I was sleeping there, and I told them about my journey of herding the cattle and my illness. They soon left me alone. After a while, a Khmer Rouge soldier came to call me to meet with the village chief of Omani. When I arrived at the house of the Khmer Rouge village chief, he questioned me about my trip. I told him what had happened to me, and he gave me some aspirin tablets to take. It was not the usual herbal medicine that was given to the people of 17 April. He was the sort of kind-hearted Khmer Rouge leader that I rarely encountered. He then told his wife to prepare food for me. I was stunned to see his wife bringing me beef soup, grilled fish and crispy cooked rice. This was the food that his family ate for lunch, and it was left over.

I would like to make it clear to my readers that the Khmer Rouge people ate only delicious and nutritious food. They did not eat watery rice-porridge with a bit of salt like us. I recently listened to an interview with the lady chef of the Khmer Rouge Foreign Minister Ieng Sary and his wife Khieu Thearith. The chef said that they enjoyed very much a meal with fried or grilled beef and roasted chicken and dessert after each meal. It was unbelievable that the Khmer Rouge leaders ate delicious food and even had servants to do their laundry! They were really hypocrites and imposters and never confessed to killing and tormenting the innocent Cambodian people before they died.

Let me go back to my story. After I took some Western medicine, ate the left-over food at the house of the Khmer Rouge village chief, I slept for a few more hours and felt better. I then thanked him and his family for their hospitality and kindness with all my heart before departing back to my village. I would like to reiterate that not all the Khmer Rouge leaders were cruel, and some had good hearts.

25: Norea Village

After I lived and worked in the Commercial Department for a few months, Ta Dek transferred me to make bricks, because in the Norea village there was a brick kiln left over from the old society. My daily job was to dig and carry the clay near the kiln, then beat, mould, and dry them in the sun. I then arranged them in the kiln and burned them with rice husks. My team leader was called "Ta Mao". He was not the usual Khmer Rouge native person. He was a 17 April (new) person like me. He was thin, tall, and very dark-skinned like a farmer/peasant. Since he was very dark, he could adapt to the situation perfectly. He made the Khmer Rouge trust him 100 percent. His running of the place was perfect. He didn't force the workers to work too hard. We slept well, ate well and had a lot of fun! The Khmer Rouge liked Ta Mao a lot because he was dark-skinned and they probably thought that he was the son of a pure peasant. The Khmer Rouge were completely deceived by Ta Mao. In fact, he had been a lieutenant in Marshall Lon Nol's army. If the Khmer Rouge had known about this, they would have killed him straightaway. However, no one reported this to the Khmer Rouge.

In front of the brick kiln was a two-storey brick house that used to belong to the original kiln owner from the old society. The brick workers slept in that brick house. At night, Ta Mao and his friends played the guitar and sang songs of the old society, not the Khmer Rouge Revolutionary Songs. Who, in the Khmer Rouge regime, would have dared to act like Ta Mao? A few of the guitar players were very good and used to perform in orchestras in the old society, before the Khmer Rouge took over the government. With more than ten people at a time, I also used to attend Ta Mao's singing party because I felt happy when I listened to songs from the old society, and I always missed my parents and siblings.

At the beginning, right after my separation from my family in April 1975, I thought that I would meet them again one day, but by 1977, I came to believe that they were all dead and I did not know where the monstrous Khmer Rouge killed them. When the Khmer Rouge killed them, they would not have buried them in a proper grave. They must have been terrified, especially my father. He was the head of the family and was cheated by the propaganda broadcast from Beijing and refused to get his family out of the country when we had the opportunity. Two of my father's sisters and one brother left for France in 1956, after the French government lost the war in Vietnam. They insisted that my father should go to France with them, but my mother refused to go because she didn't want to leave my grandmother behind.

As for my eldest sister, it was a very sad story and I'm still regretful for her loss. Her name was Sina. In 1975, she was only 19 years old and had the most beautiful face in our neighbourhood. A few suitors asked my father for her hand in marriage, but he refused them all flatly. There is one song about her which has survived to this day, titled 'Asina, Meas, Sneha, Bong!' ('Sina, my precious love!'). One person who asked my father for her hand in marriage in the early 1970s was a captain in Lon Nol's army and my father refused him as well, so he composed this song and got a famous singer, Sin Sisamuth, to sing it for him. My father did not want to allow his daughter get married to anyone, because he wanted her to marry his nephew in Marseille, France. But my father was still reluctant to send his daughter to France. By then it was too late: the Khmer Rouge took over the government and the whole country. The Khmer Rouge killed my elder sister, my grandmother, my parents, two elder brothers and maybe my youngest brother as well, but I still do not know for sure to this day because I am still searching for him, and I still have not heard any news from him. In 2002, I was in Cambodia for almost a year. I advertised in the newspaper, broadcast the news to search for him on the radio and television and I even went to the Baktra Mountain, in Pursat Province, where we separated from each other. And again in 2015, I requested the Bayon TV (their 'This Is Not A Dream' programme) to search for him, but still I did not receive any news about him. I always hope that I will hear good or bad news about him before I die.

I have deviated from my story for a while, but now I'd like to go back and continue my story in 1977. In the Norea and Samrong villages, there were 17 April people who secretly made noodles and sugar-palm cakes. If we had rice in exchange, we could exchange them for their products. There were also tailors, and if we had fabrics for them to tailor our clothes, we could do that too, in exchange for gold for their services. It appeared that living in these villages was easy and comfortable during the Khmer Rouge Regime if people had the means to do so.

By the end of 1977 and the beginning of 1978, the Southwest Region of Ta Mok's group came to occupy almost the Northwest Region. Some Khmer Rouge soldiers and local native people from the Northwest Region escaped into the forest, and the majority of them were killed by Ta Mok's group. We believe that it was karma for them. The Khmer Rouge of the Northwest Region had been killing their own people for more than two years and they, in turn, were killed by the Khmer Rouge from the Southwest Region.

In the villages, communes and districts, the Southwestern Khmer Rouge replaced most of the local leaders with their own people. Ta Dek and Ta Mao were still doing their old jobs, but under the control and surveillance of the Southwest because the Southwest thought that the Northwest was unfaithful and wanted to betray their Revolutionary Organisation. The Samrong Temple Prison was closed by the Northwest when the Southwest came to occupy it. At that time, I had a god-brother who worked as a carpenter. He entered the Samrong Temple Prison when there were no Khmer Rouge soldiers occupying it and it was vacant. He went upstairs in the wooden house where my friend and I used to sleep downstairs. When he was there, he saw a big book, he started flipping through the pages and saw all the names that were written down. There were thousands of people, and among all those names, he saw the words 'Chhuon Chhai (KT)'. KT means to destroy in Khmer, a word used by the Khmer Rouge: it literally means to kill. My god-brother is still a living witness.

26: Shingles

In January 1978, I was assigned by the Khmer Rouge to work in the rice fields in Omuni village, which was situated more than four kilometres east of the Norea village. I was still working there for a few months when I first developed shingles. At first it appeared as a cluster of small pustules on the back of my right shoulder. When the cluster of pustules was broken, it did not remain in the same place: it appeared somewhere else. I heard that if the shingles started to appear on the chest, the shingles virus would eat/ destroy the liver and cause the patient to die. I was so scared because I started to have shingles on my chest, but it did not break yet, so I went to ask the Khmer Rouge who were running the place there if I could return to the Norea village for treatment. I also heard that mung beans were effective in treating shingles. All we had to do was to chew the mung beans and apply this on the infected area and it would kill all the shingles virus. I then went to ask for some mung beans from the Southwestern Khmer Rouge member who was supervising the communal canteen. He was called Ta Kling, because he was as black as the Southern Indians. Ta Kling said to me, "No need to use mung beans, just go and get a container of water for me!"

So I went to get some water for him. The shingles had appeared on the back of my right shoulder. He then applied water on my left forearm and started slapping it hard for a while. Afterwards, several black bruises, as big as my thumb, started to appear on my forearm skin. Ta Kling then started to roll tobacco with a leaf as big as a fat cigar, and he started to light it. He inhaled it hard and blew out the smoke a few times. It was burning hot. Then he burned the apparent dark spots which he believed contained the shingles virus. He burned the black bruises again and again until I could smell the burning of my skin and flesh. I would like to thank Ta Kling for helping me cure my illness. The next day I felt the itching was gone and a few days later my shingles started to subside and stop spreading. A few weeks later, my shingles began to heal completely. I saw many shingles patients die because there was a lack of Western medicines to cure. The Khmer Rouge only manufactured by hand their traditional, herbal medicines, which they claimed that they could cure 100 different types of diseases. Their special medicines were called "Rabbit Poo" because they moulded them in the shape of rabbit poo. If we told them that we had illnesses such as headache, dizziness, diarrhoea, fever, abdominal pain, shingles and so on, we would surely be given the rabbit poo medicine. This was the most effective treatment for shingles, which was unbelievable. I would again like to thank Ta Kling – a kind-hearted Khmer Rouge member, supervising the communal canteen in the Norea village, Battambang Province, who originally came from the Southwestern region led by Ta Mok – for saving my life. I still have my shingles scars to prove my illness. Every time I touch them, I am reminded of the past which occurred in 1978, when I was almost 15 years old and living in that Communist regime, not going to school and without education and guidance. At that age I should have been raised by my parents but I wasn't lucky enough.

In 1979, when I was living in a refugee camp on the Cambodian-Thai border, I started writing for the first time in Khmer after stopping reading and writing since the fall of Phnom Penh on 17 April 1975. I had almost forgotten everything and could not write the letters, because at that time I had not even finished primary school when the Khmer Rouge took over our country. Since then, I promised myself that when I had the opportunity, I would return to school to continue my education and to continue what I had lost, which was robbed by the Khmer Rouge, especially my youth.

Can you believe that I started going to school again when I was 25 years old in Australia? I just skipped from the fifth grade/Year 5 of the elementary school/ primary school that I had not yet finished when the Khmer Rouge came to power, to the 11th grade/Year 11 and then I took the HSC (Higher School Certificate) exams at the end of Year 12, which meant that I skipped five years of studies. Do you want to know about my method or strategy? Let me tell you how I did it. Before mature-age students can study the 11th and 12th grades Baccalaureate/HSC in Australia, students must do the tests and should score at least 70% success in English and Mathematics. I first started learning English on my own in 1980, when I was a refugee in Malaysia. I just memorised words from the English-Khmer dictionary every day and practised speaking the language with foreigners whenever I had a chance. As for mathematics, I bought ten books from Grade/Year 1 to 10, because I forgot all the mathematics that I had studied in Cambodia. I tried to study Mathematics on my own without spending a cent on hiring a teacher/tutor for a full year (at that time I was still working full time in a factory) before I went to take the test. When I took the test, I got a score of 75%, which meant I got 5% more than the minimum 70% requirement. I studied hard for two full years and only stopped during bedtime. I compared that I studied three times more than other students because they studied without skipping grades for more than five years like me. When I took the Baccalaureate/ HSC exams, I passed and then I went on to study for a bachelor's degree in pure and applied mathematics and a graduate diploma in education at Macquarie University. This is not to brag that I am smart and good at studying. This was down to my determination: I did not want to break my promise that when the opportunity arose, I would study hard to succeed. When I first arrived in Australia in January 1983, many people had advised me that I would not be able to study because I was too old and had stopped studying at the age of 12 but now wanted to start school again at the age of 25, 13 years later. The probability of my success was almost nil.

The memories of the Khmer Rouge Regime of Democratic Kampuchea, 3 years, 8 months and 20 days, I will never forget until I return to the dust. Let me talk a little bit about the phrase that the Khmer Rouge often said about the Great Leap Forward. Comrade Pol Pot, also known as Saloth Sar, was the top leader of the Khmer Rouge Communist Party. He went to China quietly in the 1960s through Hanoi, Vietnam, and he met President Mao Zedong and saw him using the policies of the Great Leap Forward and the Cultural Revolution, in which President Mao closed all schools and expelled all the teachers, students and professors to work in the fields. Until the 1970s, millions of people died from starvation, overwork and disease. Comrade Pol Pot was very interested in President Mao's policy, so he started copying it blindly, because this policy in China had not been successful and many people had died. When schools, technical schools, and colleges and universities were closed, it made people ignorant, made the economy stagnant and weakened the nation. In the early 1970s, President Mao Zedong stopped using this policy and started reopening schools, but the crazy comrades Pol Pot and Ieng Sary, Pol Pot's brother-in-law, and their two wives, did not monitor the situation in China. After the overthrow of Lon Nol's government on 17 April 1975, former students who had studied in France and then became leaders of the Khmer Rouge began a policy of expelling people in cities and towns all over Cambodia to go out to work in the rice paddies empty-handed, no machinery at all, not enough supply, and most of all started killing innocent Cambodian people, their own people. They did not allow us to use Western medicines. We had to use tree roots, bark and leaves instead to cure diseases, and this caused millions of people died from preventable diseases in Cambodia!

After I was cured of shingles, the Khmer Rouge sent me back to work in the rice paddies probably they wanted to improve my knowledge, such as ploughing and harrowing the fields, broadcasting, transplanting, harvesting and threshing rice. They taught me from start to finish in the Omuni and Tapon villages.

27: Sdao Village

In June 1978, I turned 15 years old and the Khmer Rouge sent me with my friend, Thy, to Sdao village, which was about 39 km from Norea village, Rattanak Mondul district, Battambang province, on Road 57, Southwest of Battambang provincial town, because we knew how to plant rice from the start to finish. At that time my friend was 17 years old, but his body size and height were the same as mine, probably because he did not have enough food to eat. When I was sent to work on a farm in Sdao village, I felt very unhappy because I was separated from the villagers and taken away from Norea village, where I could find food to eat easily. In Sdao village, the food that they provided us was bland and not nutritious. There was no fish and no meat at all and I was tired of the work. I did not have enough sleep and had to endure strict disciplines. When I became unhappy about living and working in such bad conditions, I often kept thinking about my plans to run away. My location was then closer to the Khmer-Thai border. I learned from the elders that the Khmer-Thai border was only about 70 km away from Sdao village, and if we walked for 10 hours a day, we would reach our destination through Pailin Town in about two days. I thought about this for days, that either I had to flee to Thailand or return to Norea village. I later told my friend about my plan and he agreed. We would go back to Norea village for a while, have a good time, eat good food to improve our strength, meet many of my friends and villagers, say goodbye to all of them, then come back again to Sdao village. From there we would flee to Thailand, to run away from this brutal regime.

In the village of Norea, the Khmer Rouge broadcast propaganda news on the loudspeakers which were tied to the top of coconut trees so that the whole village could hear. We were shocked to learn of the capture and the names of the Vietnamese soldiers who had invaded Cambodia. The new ' 17 April' people of the Norea village always discussed the war between the Khmer Rouge and the Vietnamese soldiers, but I was not very interested in this war because I thought that the Khmer Rouge regime would not easily collapse and there would be no day of liberation on January 7. I did not see any Cambodian people revolting and killing the Khmer Rouge at all. Everyone was traumatised and scared of the Khmer Rouge. When the Khmer Rouge marched ex-Lon Nol soldiers to kill them in the killing fields, I didn't see them fight back at all when I was in the Chork-Kakoh village, even though they had been well trained in Thailand, and they surely knew how to wrestle, fight, and shoot efficiently. I did not see them snatch guns from the Khmer Rouge soldiers, shoot and kill them; instead, they let the Khmer Rouge tie them up and with small forest vines, which even a five-year-old child would have been able to break off. This may be because they thought that their karma was up, time for them to die, and they just made it easier for the Khmer Rouge to slaughter them like chickens. This event was witnessed by me and hundreds of other prisoners as the Khmer Rouge escorted all the former Lon Nol soldiers to be killed in a forest not far from our shed near the mouth of the river in 1976.

28: Return to Norea Village

At about three o'clock in the morning, Thy and I snuck out of the potato plantation lodge about 4 km from the main road. When we reached the road, we both hid in a bush near that road. We did not immediately start our journey to Norea village. If we walked on the national road during the day, we were afraid that the Khmer Rouge would find and capture us or they would check for our travel documents, which we didn't have. When the Khmer Rouge blew the whistle to wake everyone up to work in the morning, they would start counting people and they would find out that we were missing. They would ambush us, and if they did, they would shoot us because they considered us enemies. I was 15 years old at the time and thought to myself that I was no longer a 12-year-old boy like before, because when I was younger, the Khmer Rouge would have some sympathy for small children. Now I was big enough that they wouldn't be lenient.

On the main road, I saw bananas and potatoes being transported by tractors with large trailers. They transported them to distribute to villages, communes, and districts and they rarely gave them to us to eat. They just kept them for their own people or for the high-ranking cadre. At around 5 pm, I saw a tractor attached with a large trailer with two persons on it carrying a big load of bananas. I stopped the tractor and asked the driver where he was going. He told me that he had to transport bananas to Sala Ta On village through Norea village. He agreed to let us both ride on his trailer after I told him that I had already asked for permission to travel because my father was very sick in the village, so they let me go back to the village to visit him. The tractor driver did not ask me about my travel documents, and I did not dare ask him if he was a Khmer Rouge native person or a 17 April person like us. He drove his tractor slowly, and we both rode on a pile of bananas in the back of the trailer.

At around 9 pm, the tractor was moving closer to Norea village and we both started throwing bananas onto the sidewalk because it was quiet at night and no one was walking on the road. The driver didn't hear us throwing the bananas because of the loud noises from the engine of the tractor. We both jumped off behind the trailer, for fear that the driver would see us jump down. We did not dare to say goodbye or thank the driver. When the tractor disappeared, we hid the bananas and gave some to the villagers and my god-brothers and left some for us to eat, because bananas at that time were very valuable and people were killed for stealing them. We could even exchange them for gold. When we ate them, our body would be full of energy. The Khmer Rouge rarely let us eat them, they just kept them for their own people to eat.

When we got back to the village, we slept in an old house that was abandoned and uninhabited, and the location of that house was right next to the Sangke River. We both did not dare to report to the Khmer Rouge of our arrival in village because they knew that we did not have any parents or siblings in this village. The Southwestern Khmer Rouge of Ta Mok, who were occupying the Northwest Region, began to tighten their rule. They began to massacre people, and the Samrong Temple Prison, where I had been imprisoned, began to reopen. If anyone was arrested and imprisoned there, they would not be released. They would be crushed or killed in a banana plantation just outside the temple. We both knew the exact location of this. The Southwestern Khmer Rouge Ta Mok group were very fierce and loyal and had struggled for decades during the war. That's why the Party Leader, Pol Pot, had one hundred percent trust in them. We had both stopped working for the Khmer Rouge, and if we did not work, the Khmer Rouge would stop feeding us. During the day we slept in the abandoned house, and at night we went out to search for something to eat, otherwise we would both starve to death. We both usually went to the communal mess to search for food after midnight because the Khmer Rouge were fast asleep and their stomachs were churning with the delicious food they ate in the evening. Sometimes we could find some leftovers to eat, and sometimes we could not find anything to eat at all. We just drank water in the river and went back to sleep on the first floor of the abandoned house and our stomachs had nothing to churn like the Khmer Rouge's. The villagers that I was acquainted with knew that we had both returned to the village, but they did not know where we were hiding. I forbade my friend to tell anyone because this was a matter of life and death. To survive, we must not confide in anyone. I went to see some god-brothers of mine who were close. They were all afraid to see me: if the Khmer Rouge found out, they would be killed for collaboration with me.

The Khmer Rouge seemed angry, because they knew more about what was happening in the country than the 17 April people about the war between the Khmer Rouge and the Vietnamese Communists. The Khmer Rouge began to search in villages, communes, districts, regions, all over the country for Vietnamese residents who had been living in Cambodia for generations. They killed them all. The motto of the Khmer Rouge: "To dig the grass, one has to remove its roots." The 17 April people also knew that the Khmer Rouge were hunting for the Vietnamese. My friend, Thy, spoke fluent Vietnamese, but no one knew that he was of Vietnamese descent except me, who knew his family history very well. I met his family while living at the Champa Temple together in April 1975, before the Khmer Rouge brought them back to Phnom Penh and brutally killed his grandfather, mother and his elder sister. How could people think that the Vietnamese Communists had ordered the Khmer Rouge to kill their own people?

I had been living in this abandoned house for almost a month then and in August 1978 I planned to flee to Thailand through Sdao, Samlot and Pailin. I knew the way and I just waited for the opportunity to do so. If I continued to live like this, soon the Khmer Rouge would know our hiding place and they would capture and kill us.

In the Norea Temple at that time, the Khmer Rouge used to weave krama (meaning 'garment' or 'fabric'), and the workers in that temple were all female Khmer Rouge members from the Southwestern Region. They were dark-skinned and loyal and did not carry guns. I was surprised to learn this, but they could fight ferociously for their Communist Party. There were about 60 of them. They ate full meals and delicious food because they were the native people and not like us, the 17 April people, eating only liquefied rice porridge. One night I watched the female Khmer Rouge members, from afar, cooking two massive pots of sticky rice-banana cakes wrapped with banana leaves that made me salivate, because I had not eaten this type of sweet cake for more than three years. I did not know if they cooked for themselves or for the Khmer Rouge cadre that came to visit their garment factory. I then went back to sleep and about three o'clock in the morning, I woke up my friend, Thy, and we both felt very hungry because from the previous evening we slept without food and drank only the Sangke River water. We both started to walk quietly towards the

Norea Temple, where they were cooking those cakes in the early evening. I opened the lid and picked out a cake to taste. It was delicious. Then I found out that they cooked one pot of sticky-rice-banana cakes and the other pot was sticky-rice-pork cakes. We took almost all the cakes and only left a few for them to eat, because I felt very angry at the Khmer Rouge. They ate good food and allowed us to eat only rice porridge with mostly salt. We put all the cakes in a large hessian rice bag which could fit 100 kg of rice. I tied it up with a string and inserted a bamboo pole to carry it on our shoulders, one at the front and one at the back. It was so heavy that we both were teetering. We hid the cakes in our abandoned house and distributed more than half of them to our acquaintances and god-brothers in Norea village for them to eat with unbounded joy. Which one of you, 17 April people, ate these cakes during the Khmer Rouge/Pol Pot Era? I believe that only the Khmer Rouge made these cakes to eat among themselves!

In the morning, the Khmer Rouge discovered that they had lost two massive pots of cakes. I believed that they were shocked and wondered who dared to steal their cakes! Words passed around of the missing cakes and the whole village were very scared. The people I gave them to eat the previous night were panic-stricken. Some of them ate the rest and some buried them in the ground, for fear that the Khmer

Rouge would find out they were in possession of those cakes and they would be severely punished.

My friend and I, the next morning, ate these stolen cakes for breakfast, drank the Sangke River water, smoked rolled tobacco with the Sangke leaves, and continued our sleep, *sans-souci* about the Khmer Rouge capturing and killing us at all. The Khmer Rouge may have thought that whoever stole their cakes, their livers would be big as well. If they caught that or those thief/thieves, they would fry their livers and share the food among themselves, as I witnessed in the Samrong Temple Prison.

We ate those cakes for a few days until they were all gone and we did not go out at all. We just took a rest, relaxed a bit and waited for the situation to calm down. The fourth night after we stole those cakes, my friend and I sneaked into the Norea Temple again, and this time we stole the popular and precious Ho Chi Minh car-tyre shoes from the female Khmer Rouge residing and working in that temple. Those female Khmer Rouge slept upstairs and left their shoes at the foot of the stairs. Either they were afraid of making their lodging dirty or were afraid of being sinful, because all the temples in Cambodia once used to be sacred places and the Khmer Rouge just turned them into pigsties/ prisons/factories during their reign. I did not know which. We not only stole those shoes and put them in a large bag for us to carry, but also cut the bundles of unfinished scarves/*kra ma* that were being woven from the looms. I exchanged some of these items for rice and food, gave some to the trusted villagers and used some for myself, because the Ho Chi Minh shoes were comfortable to wear and easy to run in, like brand sport shoes nowadays. I was not greedy: as long as I my stomach was full, I was happy because I didn't know when I would be caught and killed by them.

The next day, the fierce Khmer Rouge of the Southwest Ta Mok Region were extremely angry indeed. They were very disciplined and for many years, had fought and killed hundreds of thousands of Republican soldiers, while the Republican leader Marshall Lon Nol was terrified of being captured and killed, gathered his younger second wife, children, and took the state money of one million US dollars, worth five million dollars today, and flew out of Cambodia just a few weeks before the Fall of Phnom Penh, on an American plane and spent the rest of his life comfortably in the US until the day he died. The Khmer Rouge had a great victory on 17 April 1975, but they could not locate the two young elusive thieves who had no experience in life at all!

My friend and I surprised them once again. The Khmer Rouge were very mad and tried very hard to catch us, but still they could not find our hiding spot. It was just like looking for a needle in a haystack! I was thinking hard and decided that the next day, I would leave this place. If I did not run away from this place soon I would be caught and killed for sure. The house that we were hiding was near the banks of the Sangker River, only about 20 metres from the house of the Khmer Rouge soldiers. We were hiding in plain sight in front of their eyes and noses. This was my strategy. The Khmer Rouge may think that no one dared to do like us. If they had thought long and hard, they would have realised that they once used the same strategy as us, but then they became complacent and did not pay close attention. When they were fighting with Lon Nol's soldiers and were bombed by heavy artillery, if they wanted to survive and win the battle, they had to get closer to their enemy because the mortar guns were ineffective at close range; but the Khmer Rouge forgot all about this. Maybe they were enjoying life too much, eating good food, power-hungry, and able to kill anybody they wanted. Hence they were outsmarted by two self-taught, young, inexperienced orphaned thieves!

29: Norea Village Prison

The next day, I started sleeping around 5 pm just before the sunset. I was getting a very good sleep and was not aware my friend's absence. Suddenly, I woke up around 9 pm, feeling like someone or a ghost was waking me up. And I heard the footsteps of people walking near the house where I was sleeping, and I saw my friend was being escorted by two Khmer Rouge soldiers, who were aiming their guns at him. I also saw him pointing his finger at the upper part of the house where I was sleeping. I then wanted to jump down and run away from the house to the banks of the Sangker River because it was dark and easy. Maybe I believed that the Khmer Rouge did not dare shoot me and scared off the villagers with their gunshot noises and did not know yet if we were the ones who terrorised the female Khmer Rouge members in the Norea Temple. In my old house in Phnom Penh, I used to jump down from upstairs to the ground often, and there was no problem for me because it was only about three metres tall. I once fell from the top of a coconut tree about seven metres high at the Kandal Temple in 1975 and I did not die and not a bone of mine was broken. And this house was just three metres high. But I couldn't jump!

At that time, I was hesitant and did not want to leave my friend behind, as we had been together since

1975. And during those three years, I felt like 30 years old, living and suffering in the Pol Pot's Regime. So I decided not to run, and I came downstairs willingly to the Khmer Rouge soldiers to be arrested. The Khmer Rouge then began to slap me a few times and tied me up and escorted me and my friend to a temporary prison-house in front of and on the east side of the Norea Temple. There were about 10 prisoners in the prison-house where we were taken into custody. They were not shackled. The Khmer Rouge just closed the windows and nailed pieces of wood on the outside windows so that the prisoners could not open them and escape. They just locked the front door. The prison-house was a single storey-house, with tiled floor, round pillars and corrugated iron roof sheets. The roof of the house was designed to leave a horizontal gap of about twenty centimetres for ventilation. Readers may be familiar with the traditional village houses that are built in this way, because it is easy to ventilate and cool the house naturally without the use of air conditioners.

I had lived in this village for more than a year and did not know that there was a prison-house just in front of the Norea Temple at all. I used to walk past the front of this house hundreds of times and I didn't notice it at all, and then I thought that the Khmer Rouge were so good at hiding things in plain sight. I did not know that Pol Pot or Saloth Sar was an important person and the Party Secretary; even my father did not know about him either. He just assumed that Dr. Khieu Samphan, who received a PhD from France, was the Secretary of the People's Communist Party. We, Khmers, had been deceived by Pol Pot big time, who caused millions of people to die all over the country.

When the two of us were taken inside the prison-house, I immediately saw more than a dozen inmates sitting against the wall in silence. I then looked at the layout of the prison-house. It had two smooth round pillars with wooden beams and no ceiling. The house was about five metres high, and with those round and smooth pillars, if anyone knew how to climb, he could go out through the space between the roofs that was left for ventilation easily. I just looked at them momentarily, and I knew for sure that there was a way to escape, but I kept it to myself did not dare to tell anyone even my close friend, Thy.

In the next morning, a few young Khmer Rouge soldiers, armed with guns, opened the door and walked into the prison-house. They just stood in front of us and started kicking each of us in the head several times. I did not answer, did not cry, did not scream for my mother for help and did not even feel any pain at all. It was just as if my body was anaesthetised. The young soldiers shouted at us, "Are you condemned two the ones who stole two massive pots of banana and pork sticky rice cakes?", "Did the condemned two of you steal the *kra ma*/scarves from the looms in the Norea Temple?", "Did you two condemned thieves steal from our female fellow soldiers, the Ho Chi Minh rubber shoes and terrorise them in the past few weeks?". I just shook my head and said no adamantly. The Khmer Rouge soldier kids started kicking me and my friend again and again, and all of a sudden, they walked out, without saying anything further, and just locked the door behind them.

The other prisoners, who were older than I, and were sitting next to me, were terrified, and silent. Perhaps they did not know when they would be tortured like me next. I also looked at my friend and shook my head. I couldn't utter any words about his stupidity. He may have realised that he had made a serious and fatal mistake. He was careless, and as a result, he lead the Khmer Rouge to our hiding spot, and this time, I was sure that the Khmer Rouge soldiers would kill both of us. The Khmer Rouge would kill any person without mercy, if that person tried to destroy their Organisation, such as cutting the *kra ma*/scarves that were being woven from the looms, making it very difficult for the female Khmer Rouge to re-attach and continue weaving because the threads were jumbled up. For more than three years then, the Khmer Rouge Organisation had been brainwashing, training and educating us how to farm efficiently, to adapt to their society, to eat liquid rice porridge with salt, and every time we got sick, we would get the cure-it-all, traditional herbal medicine; but still we did not follow their paths/teachings. This time, the Khmer

Rouge Communist Organisation had to destroy us because their saying at that time went like this: "To keep you is not profitable, to remove you is not lost."

This was not for the first time that I was arrested because of my friend's feeble-mindedness and silliness. When we entered the Provincial Town of Battambang for the first time in 1975, he went, without consulting me, to ask for food in the canteen from the Khmer Rouge's kitchen staff who catered for the Communist Chinese experts/advisers near the train station and was subsequently arrested by the Khmer Rouge. He then led them to arrest me while I was sleeping soundly with an empty stomach in our hiding spot. The second time, when we travelled from the Chork-Kakoh village to near Anlong Vil village, I asked my friend to wait for me under the sugar palm tree and keep watch for the Khmer Rouge while I climbed up the tree to collect the sugar palm juice. If he saw the Khmer Rouge approaching, he should alert me, and I would hurriedly descend from the top of the tree and ran, so that they could not arrest us. But it was not like that: the Khmer Rouge was waiting to arrest me under the palm tree. And when I descended from the tree top and reached the ground, my friend was nowhere to be seen and I did not know where he went. Then I saw him coming out of the nearby banana plantation where he was hiding, because he saw the Khmer Rouge arrested me for stealing the sugar palm juice. He probably did not want be separated from me since we had been struggling together since 1975. So I concluded that my friend went to hide in the banana plantation as soon as he saw the Khmer Rouge approaching and felt scared, maybe even urinated in his pants.

At around 9 am the same day, before the Khmer Rouge summoned me for questioning, I whispered to my friend not to confess anything at all, despite being tortured, and he nodded in agreement. The Khmer Rouge summoned him first for questioning in another room. I was shocked when I heard him shouting, "Oh mother, help me, I'm in very bad pain! Please help your dearest child!" He howled for his dear mother for help in agony. The whole prison-house was filled with his screams because this house was small, and we could hear any sound a person made. The prisoners sitting in a line against the wall next to me were also terrified. The Khmer Rouge beat and tortured my poor friend for more than an hour, then they brought him out of the interrogation room, and I saw him limping badly. Maybe he needed someone to make him steady, and he looked as if he had just recovered from a severe illness. I did not ask him the reasons he was being tortured because the Khmer Rouge soldiers were standing nearby.

Then, once it was my turn, I was called to walk into the interrogation room and the door was closed behind me. When I saw a dynamo I was surprised because I was from Phnom Penh, and I knew exactly what a dynamo was. A dynamo for a bicycle is a device that, when we spin its head fast, the wires that connect it to the dynamo generate electricity. When we touch the electric current, it will shock us like an electric shock. For example, when its head is spun against the rim of the wheel as when we ride a bicycle, it produces electricity, and if we connect it to a lamp, it illuminates the road when we ride it at night. But this was not a bicycle dynamo. It was probably a car dynamo because it was as big as an adult's thigh. I saw the Khmer Rouge attach a black rubber belt to the dynamo, and the black rubber belt was also attached to the rim of the bicycle wheel, and they spun the wheel and wired it to the dynamo. And when the Khmer Rouge spun it, it produced electric sparks. This dynamo was about 20 to 30 times stronger than a small bicycle dynamo. At first, the Khmer Rouge did not shock me immediately, they just spun the dynamo and it gave sparks. They asked me questions casually, as if they were compassionate and close to me. At that time my body was still small because I did not have enough meat, vegetables and fruits to eat and hence my height and size could not grow like a normal child with enough food to eat. My body was deficient in vitamins and proteins, even though I was 15 years old at the time. As for my friend, he was 17 years old and his body was as small as mine. I told my interrogator that I came from the potato plantation in the village-district of Sdao and I just arrived the previous night. I asked a tractor driver carrying bananas for a lift from Sdao village and I arrived in this village for less than two hours before I was arrested. I whispered how to answer the questions to my friend the night before. If we gave them the same story, the Khmer Rouge would be doubtful that we were guilty. I also told him that I had already asked the chief of Sdao village for permission to come back to the village and find some herbal medicines to treat malaria, because in Sdao village, there were a lot of malaria cases. He then asked whether there was no distribution of anti-malarial drugs there. I wanted to reply to him that their traditional medicines called "rabbit poo" were not effective, because when I had a headache, stomach ache, diarrhoea, or fever, they gave me the same medicine. The Khmer Rouge often said that their famous "rabbit poo medicines" were very effective, they could cure 100 illnesses. But I did not answer in this way to the Khmer Rouge, because I was afraid he would be angry with me. Instead I replied that I came to visit this village because I missed the villagers and close friends very much. He also started to ask about my friend, whether he had stolen any banana and pork sticky rice cakes from the Norea Temple a week ago. I immediately replied to him that it was impossible. The rice cakes had been missing for more than a week and we both just arrived last night for the first time. He was silent for a moment and then asked me about the loss of food in the communal mess, the loss of dozens of Ho Chi Minh's rubber shoes, the damage of the looms by cutting off the threads of the *kra ma*/scarves, which were being woven, the theft of the *kra ma*/scarves from the looms and above all the scaring of 60 female Khmer Rouge members in the Norea Temple. I was observing that my interrogators were surely using a good cop/bad cop negotiation strategy. I did not know where they learned this technique from. As for me, I did not even finish primary school, but I knew their technique instinctively. When the good cop strategy was not achieved, they started to use the bad cop strategy. They then started kicking and punching me. They did not tie my hands, maybe they saw that I was small and they just let me sit on the brick floor and beat the hell out of me. They beat me and asked me again, but I still said I did not know. It wasn't us, and it was impossible, because the day they lost the cakes and the day we arrived was one week apart. Then, they began beating me again and again until I was exhausted. He then started spinning the dynamo and shocked me, and as a result I started to have convulsions on the tile floor, but I did not shout or scream for help. I knew that they wouldn't shock me to death because they were still doubtful and they didn't have any hard evidence. They did this many times, but they still did not achieve their goal because my little body was no longer in pain and it was as if I was under anaaesthetic. After being tortured for more than an hour, I was sent back to my sleeping area. At noon, we and the other prisoners were given liquid rice porridge with a few pinches of salt, and I gulped it down in one go. In the afternoon, they beat me and my friend again, but still did not get the answers they wanted. The next day, the Khmer Rouge beat us twice more and still did not achieve their goal. They then told us that they would send us to the Samrong Temple Prison the next day. I did not reply to them at all and I did not tell them that I was a former prisoner of the Samrong Temple Prison more than a year ago. I whispered to my friend that after midnight, we would have to escape from this prison-house. If we didn't do it that night, and when we got to the Samrong Temple Prison, they would shackle us and we would not be able to survive because we knew their interrogation techniques, such as pulling off toenails, etc., and we would admit everything! We also knew that the Southwest Ta Mok Khmer Rouge were very thorough in their work. When the prisoners were taken inside the prison, they would not release them at all. It was just a one-way ticket for them!

30: Fishing along the Sangker River

At about two am in the next morning, I whispered to Thy that I would climb up the pillar and escape first and would wait for him at the potato garden patch outside. If after half an hour I did not see him come out, I would leave alone. I thought that my friend could not climb the pillar because the pillars of the house were smooth and slippery, and I had never seen him climb a palm tree ever since I had known him for more than three years. I was the one who could climb trees and picked fruits for him to eat. In the Chork-Ka-koh village, there were no coconut trees because they were isolated from the actual villages. There were only sugar-palm trees. No matter how smooth the trunks of the sugar-palm trees were, I could always climb them if I wanted. I did not need to use a rope attached to my ankles for gripping the tree-trunk to prevent slipping and to push my body upwards. I began to climb the pillar of the house quietly, and was afraid that the other prisoners sleeping would hear me and begin shouting in panic and to alert the Khmer Rouge soldiers guarding outside. During the Khmer Rouge Regime, I had also seen a lot of people denouncing others for their advantages and they didn't care if the ones they denounced were killed or not.

When I reached the wooden beams, I just crawled

on them to the gap in the air vents on the roof because this house had no ceiling. Once I reached the space between the roofs of the house, I put one foot out first, then followed with my hand. I leaned over and lay down through the gap for ventilation, because the gap was about six to seven metres long, from one corner of the wall to the other, and I pushed my body out. When I reached the roof of the house covered with galvanised iron sheets, I stood up and started walking on the roof. I did not know in advance that there were Khmer Rouge soldiers guarding the area outside. The Khmer Rouge had torches using dynamos instead of batteries pointing towards the roof of the house where I had made a sound. I lay flat on the roof immediately to avoid being seen by them because they were holding AK-47 rifles. If they saw me escaping, they would shoot me immediately, because we 17 April/ new people were worthless to them and they treated us worse than animals. I lay still for a while, and when it was quiet, I started walking again, and the Khmer Rouge started using their torches again. Near that prison-house there was a coconut tree and its branches were lying on the roof of the house, and maybe they thought that the wind was blowing the coconut-tree branches on the corrugated iron roof and making noises. So I prostrated myself as before. I started to walk on the coconut-tree branch and reached the top of the coconut tree very easily. From there, I just climbed down to the ground without much effort.

When I reached the ground, I hid in a garden patch of potatoes waiting for my friend, who was still inside, to come out. I waited for him for more than half an hour and did not see him coming out, so I decided to leave him behind, because I was afraid that the Khmer Rouge would arrest me and endanger my life. As I was about to leave my best friend, I suddenly heard footsteps on the roof of the house and saw the Khmer Rouge flashlights. I saw my friend crouching down for a while, then I saw him starting to walk again and jump from the rooftop to the ground, making a loud noise. He certainly did not walk along the coco-nut-tree branch and climbed down quietly like me, he just jumped down to the ground immediately without having to wait long. I got out of the garden patch of potatoes and held his hands, because I was very happy that he was able to escape from that prison-house. I did not want to leave him behind and was afraid he would be killed. Then, I hurriedly released his hands and we ran as fast as we could to the banks of the Sangke River. There was a small fishing boat that had been tied up. I suddenly untied the boat and then we started to row it with one oar each towards the City of Battambang, and then we continued on to the Khveng Temple, just beyond the Tamim Temple because the Khveng Temple was isolated and far away from the eyes of the Khmer Rouge and the other villagers. We then tied the boat to rest until dawn.

At that time, I could only row the boat sitting with a

small oar and did not know how to row standing with a big and long oar, tied by a piece of string with a short stick attached to the edge of the boat for long distances (rowlock). Fortunately, on my boat, there were different kinds of fishing nets. Maybe this fishing boat belonged to the Khmer Rouge, or their families or the communal mess, I didn't know. In the next morning, we both fished with the nets along the Sangke River. We caught a lot of fish because the river at the time teemed with fish, then we went up to the bank to grill them and ate them with great pleasure. Along the Sangker River, the Khmer Rouge soldiers did not go down to the bank to check for fishing permits, because they just assumed that the fishermen along the Sangke River were fishing for their communal villages. I never talked to those fishermen along the Sangke River. I was afraid of being questioned about which communal mess I fished for and getting reported to the Khmer Rouge. Thy and I both ate grilled fish only and drank the river water, but we lacked plates, pots, pans and above all, rice.

In August 1978, after few days spent on the boat, I quickly learnt how to row it standing up. I paddled, threw my left leg back and forth, and pushed the oar forward, because I saw other fishermen rowing like that. I did not need to be taught how to row a boat in a standing position: I just observed other fishermen rowing their boats and copied them.

One night, at about two o'clock in the morning, the

two of us tied our boat on the bank of the river, under a big tree, just outside the main hospital in the Battambang Provincial Town. During that time the Khmer Rouge called it "Hospital P1". We just walked up from the shore into the hospital. This hospital was set up for the Khmer Rouge cadre members, children and soldiers, exclusively for treating only them. If new/ 17 April people like us were sick, the Khmer Rouge would leave us to die. They would not take us to this main hospital. Very rarely, only a few 17 April people, with possible connections with the Khmer Rouge, would be admitted to this hospital. I heard that there were doctors imported from the Communist China working in this hospital, treating only the Khmer Rouge cadre.

By the time we arrived at this hospital, it was quiet. All the staff, including, doctors, nurses, patients and the kitchen staff were all asleep soundly with full stomachs. We roamed the hospital for a period of time because we did not know the layout and we never been admitted. Even though I had been suffering from malaria for months and almost died in the Chak village and had shingles for more than a month and nearly died from it as well, I was never taken to this hospital. This was the first time I came here. I only saw this hospital from the river when I was rowing the boat. We walked up and down and found a medical dispensing room and a mess, and next to the mess was a warehouse. When I opened the door of the warehouse, it was as if I had seen a treasure trove of gold and silver. It stocked sugar, rice, salt, dried fish from the Tonle Sap freshwater lake and other things. I started to take rice, salt, dried fish and sugar, then put it in a large sack of rice and carried it on my shoulder. As for my friend, he collected plates, spoons and pots. We could certainly survive for at least a few more weeks. Then we left the hospital and went back to the boat and paddled it back to the Khveang Temple safely because this area was quiet and away from the eyes of the people and the Khmer Rouge. As for the main hospital, there were no Khmer Rouge guards, so it was easy for us to get in and out.

When we were bored, we just rowed the boat along the Sangke River up and down to see the scenery, just like tourists normally do. Who wanted to work for the Khmer Rouge, who did not pay us any salaries, who did not give us enough food to eat, who did not give us medicines when we were sick, and above all did not allow us to go to school? They certainly wanted us to be illiterate so that they could control us easily and we would not be able to use our intelligence to fight back. They also made us work worse than slaves from the Angkorean Period and made us orphans.

We rowed our boat upstream along the banks of the Sangker River, and there were and still exist today many temples such as the Sampov Temple, Kor Temple, Tamim Temple, Khveng Temple, Kampong Seima Temple, Kampong Pil Temple, Slor Kram Temple, Khsach Pouy Temple, Chheu Teal Temple,

Bay Damram Temple, Banan Temple. We even went to the Kantue and Krahot villages. When we were tired, we just slept on the river banks and we were happy. We lived in our boat for two months and then sneaked back into the village of Norea quietly to observe the situation in the village and also brought some fish to distribute to the people in the village. The villagers said that the Khmer Rouge started to tighten their grips on the people; perhaps their era was ending soon.

The two of us also rowed our boat downstream along the banks of the Sangke River, and we observed the temples along the river, such as the Sangke Temple, Kandal Temple, Po Veal Temple, Leap Temple, Sophy Temple, Ballat Temple, Romduol Temple, Slaket Temple, Norea Temple, Kdol Daun Teav Temple, Keo Temple, Kdang Ngea Temple, Sampov Meas Temple, Daun Keo Temple, Moha Suong Temple, Bak Amrek Village, Daun Mea Village, Reach Daun Keo Village, Prek Trop Village and Bak Prea Village. When we ran out of rice and other things, we just went to the warehouse in the P1 Hospital in town to collect our supplies.

Around October 1978, I got into a bit of an argument with my partner because he was not very careful. He started sneaking back into Norea village often and I believed that it could jeopardise my safety. So he found another boat and we parted ways with sadness because we had been together for more than three years then. One evening, I tied up my boat on the bank of the Sangker River next to the new stone bridge. The Khmer Rouge saw me having caught a lot of fish, and they asked me for some of my fish, and I replied to them that if they had any tobacco, I would be able to trade it for my fish. Then they disappeared for a while and came back with a large amount of tobacco in exchange for my fish. They probably thought that I was a legal fisherman fishing for the communal mess. But, in fact, I was just a simple petty thief, trying to survive and dodging working for the Khmer Rouge for free, on the Sangke River. After I and my long time-friend had been parted our ways, I found a male orphan and brought him to live on my boat with me. The orphan's name was called Ruy, translated literally as "House Fly". I called him "A Ruy". He was about 10 years old, polite and obedient. His belly was protruding, maybe swollen, and his ribs were showing. He was badly malnourished and starving. If I hadn't taken him in, he would have died, for sure, because he didn't work for the Khmer Rouge, hence no food was given to him. I fed him pure rice, fresh fish from the river and fruits every day for about a month, then his health was almost back to normal.

As November 1978, was approaching, the situation in Cambodia became increasingly tense. The villagers said that the Khmer Rouge were getting angrier and angrier. They broadcast, on loudspeakers transmitted from the radio, about the war between the Khmer Rouge and the Vietnamese soldiers and said that they had won every battle against the Vietnamese enemy, but their faces showed otherwise. They seemed scared and under severe stress. By December 1978, I heard from the villagers that the Khmer Rouge were rounding people up and taking them to the Samrong Temple Prison, but all those prisoners were never seen coming back out alive.

In the fourth week of December 1978, I saw the Khmer Rouge soldiers along with their families fleeing from the surrounding villages and making their ways along National Road 5 to the west towards Thailand. As I rowed my boat through the Battambang Provincial Town, I saw thousands of Khmer Rouge people all over the town of Battambang, and each truck was full of people. Maybe they wanted to flee to Thailand for safety from the attacks of the Vietnamese army.

I parked my boat at the Sala Ta On village and let my adopted brother, A Ruy, look after it. I walked back to Norea village, then I went to the Samrong Temple Prison, because the Khmer Rouge army had already run away. I heard the villagers said that, before the Khmer Rouge fled west, they threw a few hand grenades inside the building where the prisoners were still shackled inside, with the intention of killing them all. But when I arrived there, I found dozens of prisoners were still alive inside the building. I saw some dead bodies from when the Khmer Rouge threw their hand grenades. I immediately went looking for a few of my acquaintances from the village to help me break the door of the prison open so that all the prisoners could run away from this hell-hole. In a blink of an eye, all the prisoners ran away like a herd of cows in a panic. Some of them fell down and recovered. Maybe they were exhausted, because they had eaten only small portions of watery porridge with salt. They probably thought that they were being rescued by an unknown god, who provided them with full energy and they were able to run as strong as the fully-fed cattle, and that someone had come to save them from their imminent deaths. In fact, that person or saint or god was an orphan and his revolutionary name was called "Comrade Sau". His parents, grandmother and several of his siblings were brutally killed by the Khmer Rouge, and particularly, he was the youngest former porridge cook at the Samrong Temple Prison. One particular prisoner among all those who escaped is now currently a Parliamentarian in the Siem Reap Province. His name is His Excellency Seang Nam. In the past decade, I reconnected with him and I saw with my own eyes that he built hundreds of roads for the people to use for free with his own money. He even built a building in the Siem Reap mosque for the Khmer Muslims, and he is my living witness.

On 10 January 1979, I saw the Vietnamese army and the army of the National Salvation Front of Samdech Decho Hun Sen, our current Prime Minister, arriving in Battambang Province. I would like to thank Samdech Decho Hun Sen, the army of the National

Salvation Front and the Vietnamese army for coming to the rescue of our country and our Cambodian people in time. If they didn't come in time, I would surely have died at the hands of the Khmer Rouge and I wouldn't have been able to write this story.

After the prisoners escaped from the prison, that very night, the Khmer Rouge returned. They entered the Samrong Temple Prison, perhaps because they wanted to kill all of them. When they arrived, they did not see any prisoners; they only saw that the doors were broken and unlocked, and that there were some dead bodies. Then they immediately left the prison for fear of being killed by the National Salvation Front. I was informed by some villagers residing near the prison about this. I was definitely not there, because my duty was over and I did not want the Khmer Rouge to kill me, even though they killed my grandmother in April 1957, when she was 75 years old. My father was 52 years old, my mother was 35 years old, my sister was 19 years old, my two brothers were 17 and 15 years old, and probably my youngest brother was 8 years old. I am still looking for him after more than 46 years, but I still haven't heard from him at all.

31: 7 January 1979

All the rice warehouses in the Battambang Province were broken into by the starving people because the Khmer Rouge had already fled to the forest. When I got back to my boat, I did not see my adopted brother there at all. All I saw were my fish nets and rice. He had already left. Maybe he waited for me for too long. We have never seen each other again up to this day.

I traded my fish nets and boat for gold with the other fisherman. I kept that gold for my future because it was the currency at the time and I could barter it for anything I wanted. I believed that I might have a good chance to flee to Thailand then. People were rushing into the Battambang Provincial Town after the Khmer Rouge left. They picked up items such as motorbikes, speakers, generators, batteries, etc. The villagers were very happy. They played music on the recently acquired cassette players and danced all over the villages with great joy. I also obtained a bicycle when I entered the town after the Khmer Rouge fled. Later, I traded my bicycle for an old blue Vespa motorcycle with a round headlight. I traded my gold for gasoline with the Vietnamese army, and I rode the motorcycle all over the villages and the Battambang Provincial Town. Riding it was just like riding on an airplane. I felt very happy then, but my happiness could not last forever. All good things must come to an end.

32: Travel to Thailand

In February 1979, I heard from other people that my younger sister, who had been separated from me at the Kampong Chhnang port in 1975, was still alive. She went by train, which stopped at the Thip-adei Mountain (Phnom Ta Pde) railway station. The Khmer Rouge sent her to farm in the Koh Kralor district, Battambang Province. I also found two other families, on my father's side. I invited my friend, Thy, to live with us and we planned to travel to Thailand together. In total, there were 14 of us, and we took the National Road 5 towards the Serey Sophorn Town and continued our journey to Poipet. We gave some gold to the guides to take us through the forest to the Thai-Cambodian border. We crossed the border into Thailand and resided in the Nong Chan refugee camp. Travelling from the Battambang Provincial Town to the Thai-Cambodian border took us three days. The 14 of us stayed in the Nong Chan refugee camp for almost three weeks.

At around 9 o'clock in the morning at the Nong Chan refugee camp, before the Thai government sent the refugees back to Cambodia, dozens of buses were lined up and they put signs on the windshields of the buses for USA, France, China, Malaysia and other countries. The Thai government did this to divert our attention so that we would not revolt or flee back to

Cambodia. They actually used the same tricks as the Khmer Rouge. Maybe they learned from the Khmer Rouge, no one knew. All the refugees, including my group of 14, had to get on board that would transport us to one of those foreign countries. Our group got in the wrong bus and all the people on board were Cambodians of Chinese descent. They were apparently waiting to leave for China, and they all looked happy. They chased us out of the bus and said to us, "You Cham people/Khmer Muslims have to get on another bus for Malaysia. This is our bus which will take us to China." We apologised to the Chinese and got off the bus and got on the apparently correct bus for Malaysia. From the Nong Chan refugee camp to the Dangrek Mountains, near the Preah Vihear temple, is only 334 km, but we were transported from 9 am to 5 am the next day, which meant that we travelled by bus for 20 hours. We stopped for refuelling only because the Thai government wanted to trick and divert us.

When all the refugees arrived on the Dangrek Mountains, the Chinese and Cham brothers and sisters met again. We just looked at one another and shook our heads. We didn't say anything and we all thought that we were tricked by the Thai government! After we reached the edge of the Dangrek Mountain, the Thai soldiers shot into the air to scare us and make us hurry down the mountain back into the Khmer territory. The mountain was high and steep. Some old people who could not walk were left to die in the middle of mountain while descending. As people started to descend the mountain, a lot of them stepped on landmines that the Khmer Rouge had deployed. These exploded, cutting off their limbs and killing them instantly. All the 14 of us were very lucky and did not step on any landmines.

When we got to the foot of the Dangrek Mountain, we all stopped to cook our lunch and rest on the bank of a stream. Some people went to bathe in the stream and others went to fetch water to cook. Suddenly, someone stepped on a mine planted by the Khmer Rouge. It was a deadly explosion, and we saw blood floating red in the stream. None of the 14 of us were killed or injured by landmines, but other people were injured and killed. It was so sad, because they survived the Khmer Rouge regime, only to die near their destinations!

We travelled on foot during the day and slept during the night. While we were travelling and resting, we were all the time guarded and escorted by the Vietnamese soldiers, perhaps because they were afraid the Khmer Rouge would take the people with them. The Vietnamese soldiers also distributed noodles and flour for us to cook and eat.

My group of 14 people walked for seven days straight before we reached the Provincial Town of Kampong Thom and then we boarded the Vietnamese army truck back to Phnom Penh safely.

Epilogue

This is just one section of my autobiography. I don't really know if I could complete my full story, only time will tell!

I finished writing this story on Monday, 23:52 hours, 21 December 2020. I finished writing it in just five days.